SALERATUS

The World's Greenest Chemical
The World's Greenest Chemical

The Curious History & Complete Uses
of

BAKING SODA

Peter A. Ciullo

MARADIA PRESS
NAUGATUCK, CT

Copyright © 1994 by Peter A. Ciullo

This book is available at quantity discounts for educational and promotional uses.

Publisher's Cataloging In Publication
(Prepared by Quality Books Inc.)

Ciullo, Peter A., 1954-
      Saleratus : the curious history & complete uses of baking soda / Peter A. Ciullo
      p. cm.
      Includes bibliographical references and index.
      Preassigned LCCN: 93-80791
      ISBN 0-9626043-9-9

      1. Sodium bicarbonate.   I. Title

   TP245.S7C58 1994   661'.323
                                           QBI93-22460

Printed in the United States of America

Dedication

In memory of Josephine Ciullo, Ida DeCiampis and Alice Arcari, who brought dignity and love to good food and a clean home.

Acknowledgements

Thanks, above all, to my family - Claudia, Marissa and Adam.

A special debt of gratitude is owed John Pote, for giving me the idea, and Jerry Reen, for sharing his historical perspective.

Many thanks, as well, for the help and advice of the Hoffman family, Chris Lemmond, Tom Whitney, Dr. Wayne Sorenson, Steve Lajoie and Dr. William Jensen.

CONTENTS

INTRODUCTION

FROM ACID STOMACH TO ACID RAIN

A book about baking soda? Baking soda would seem about as compelling a topic as club soda. It is, nevertheless, as uniquely American as Coney Island hot dogs or corn-on-the-cob. The use of baking soda in the refrigerator, or to clean everything from battery terminals to teeth, was not the invention of Madison Avenue. Nearly all of the popular uses of baking soda - a.k.a. sodium bicarbonate, bicarbonate of soda, bicarb, and soda - in the Helpful Hints columns were developed by American consumers over the past 150 years. Its general use in the kitchen and its eventual use in every other room in the house (plus the garage) is a paradigm of American ingenuity and pioneer spirit. Here is a simple, cheap food ingredient for which the American people conceived some unusual, certainly unintended, but nonetheless ingenious folk uses.

No one knows who first thought of putting baking soda in the refrigerator to absorb odors. But it worked and was a common practice long before a major manufacturer, with no little skepticism, launched a costly program to discover just how effective it was. And who has not on occasion brushed his or her teeth with baking soda when the toothpaste ran out? It wasn't minty and it wasn't sweet, but it worked. Now baking soda is to toothpaste marketing of the 90's what fluoride was in the 50's.

In North America, the home uses of baking soda surpassed simply baking long ago. In the rest of the world, baking soda remains a kitchen oddity. Where available, it is used almost strictly as an antacid. Industrial uses, on the other hand, have proliferated globally. In addition to packaged foods, sodium bicarbonate is used in blood dialysis, animal feeds, fire extinguishers, textile processing, oil well drilling muds, carpet cleaners, foam rubber, denture cleaners and paint strippers, among other things. True to its tradition as a safe and natural ingredient for a healthy home environment, baking soda's unique attributes are now being broadly applied to controlling toxic metals in drinking water, improving waste treatment processes, and reducing the acid in smoke stack emissions.

Baking soda is unquestionably an eminently natural ingredient. As sodium bicarbonate, it is available in virtually endless supply. It occurs in the minerals trona and nahcolite, in briney lakes and in lake sediments. The bicarbonate content of the oceans plays a key role in stabilizing the carbon dioxide content of the earth's atmosphere. Likewise, sodium bicarbonate is essential to the functioning of the human body. It helps to maintain the proper acid/alkaline balance of blood. It is the major vehicle of carbon dioxide transport from body tissue to the lungs. It is a primary component of the duodenal fluid that neutralizes stomach contents before they enter the intestinal tract. Sodium bicarbonate is also a component of saliva where it helps to reduce the attack of orally generated acids on tooth enamel.

Sodium bicarbonate, because of its fundamental safety and efficacy, is widely used in food and pharmaceuticals, of course, but is now also ingested in very small amounts via baking soda toothpastes and certain potable water supplies. This increased consumption has, understandably, not come without concern over its sodium component. Despite the essential nature of both the sodium and bicarbonate ions to human physiology, baking soda has elicited the expected attention in regard to use by hypertensive individuals. Research over the past decade, however, has suggested that it is salt, sodium plus chloride, not just sodium per se that can aggravate hypertension. Various studies with animals and humans have indicated that salt sensitive hypertensives will show clinically increased blood pressure in response to sodium chloride but not other sodium salts, including the bicarbonate. Much more research is, nevertheless, required before the medical community reassesses its position on sodium intake by salt sensitive individuals.

Most of the world's supply of sodium bicarbonate is made primarily from salt, limestone and coal, while all U.S. production is by the conversion and purification of the minerals trona and nahcolite. Although it exists as an abundant natural resource, baking soda depends on sophisticated processing to meet the stringent standards of quality and purity mandated for most of its many uses. This type of beneficial amalgam of nature and technology may well be a worthy model for our times. In the current age of acute environmental and ecological awareness, when chemicals are suspect and natural is preferred, baking soda has managed to transcend the political as possibly the world's "greenest" chemical.

□ □ □ □ □

This book is composed of five sections designed to be read in succession, but which can be equally well appreciated individually according to the particular interests of the reader.

Section 1 is historical in nature, presenting the rise of baking soda as a household staple intertwined with the industrial and commercial development of the United States. This is where you'll learn what "saleratus" means and how it relates to today's baking soda. Heady stuff maybe, if your interest is mainly in a way to clean your bathroom sink, but it will certainly lend a new perspective on how baking soda progressed from pancakes to porcelain.

Section 2 is what originally motivated the writing of this book, although it has ended up blazing trails in baking soda lore farther and wider than originally envisioned. This is the section where nearly all of the "folk" uses of baking soda have been compiled for the first time, as far as we know. If you're wondering what else you can do with baking soda besides brushing teeth and cleaning battery terminals, you've picked the right book. The collection of uses is comprehensive, but of necessity not strictly complete. Several of the uses suggested over the past century or so have been more imaginative than effective. Others have not been without the potential for some degree of peril.

Section 3 covers in detail three of the more prominent commercial uses of baking soda. Two of these are taken for granted, while the third is one you've probably never heard of before - and it's the biggest single use worldwide.

Section 4 covers the industrial uses where the familiar household benefits of baking soda have been applied to no less a task than cleaning the environment. You'll discover how baking soda is being used to make the air we breathe, the water we drink and even the ground we walk on cleaner and safer.

Section 5 is the Appendix to the book proper, concentrating on one specific use of baking soda - baking. After all, what would a book on baking soda be without recipes? The Appendix is more than just cupcakes and muffins, though. It is a short course on the ingredients you use in baking every day, and just how they conspire with baking soda to such delicious ends.

Is this book everything you ever wanted to know about baking soda? Most likely, it's more than you ever suspected you could.

ONE

Baking

Soda

Rises

What does that arm and hammer logo stand for, and how did it end up on all those baking soda boxes? (see page 18)

ONE

BAKING SODA RISES

The growth of baking soda in America began, naturally enough, with baking. Although known and used by the medical community, its foothold in American homes was based on its use as a leavening agent. This was an outgrowth of the art and science of baking as it developed from colonial days until the commercial introduction of saleratus, as baking soda was then known, in the early 1800's.

Before baking soda, bakers leavened with brute force or with natural yeasts. Raised baked goods resulted from tedious hand beating to incorporate air bubbles or from the carbon dioxide liberated by yeasts. Yeasts were a lot less work. From ancient times, these yeasts were obtained literally from thin air, as for sourdoughs, or were prepared from beer fermentation by-products.

The first American colonists brought from Europe both traditional baking skills and an inbred distrust of water as a beverage. For the most part, the limited availability of truly potable water in the initial settlement of the Northeast did little to correct this predjudice. Brewing for beverage and for baking became a priority. Unfortunately, the New England soils and climate were not friendly to barley and hops. A traditional beer had to await the settlement of the more agriculturally hospitable

Pennsylvania. Not easily discouraged, the early colonists soon improvised equally satisfying, or at least equally potent, brews from pumpkins, persimmons, apples and maple sugar. Each source of "beer" meant a yeast source for baking.

By the close of the 18th century, pumpkin beer, and pumpkin-yeast bread were faded memories to the citizens of the cosmopolitan East, but the ability to brew beer and extract yeast from unusual sources remained a valuable skill to the westward bound settlers. Beer yeast and sourdough baked goods established their distinct culinary niches based on the location, circumstances and tastes of the baker. It was a solution to sourdough sourness which ultimately led to an alternative to yeast itself, and prepared the way for baking soda.

THE PEARLASH EVOLUTION

From the earliest colonial settlements, potash was an economic staple in the colonies. Potash, crude potassium carbonate made from wood ash, was a necessary ingredient for making both soap and glass. By the mid-18th century, the production of potash had grown from a cottage industry to a major commercial enterprise in tandem with the corresponding development of soap and glass manufacture. A purer, more concentrated form of potash, known as pearlash, had also become a common raw material for these industries. While potash typically contained from 5% to 25% potassium carbonate, pearlash contained between 70% and 95%, and sold at a corresponding premium.

The production of colonial potash and pearlash was given a boost in 1750 by the mother country. England had become highly dependent upon Russian potash for its industrial needs, having already seriously depleted the forests of Great Britain for the production of wood ash. A politically motivated potash embargo, declared by the Czar, forced England to turn to her colonies. Within four years, the American colonies, with trees to burn, had nullified the Russian embargo with both potash and premium pearlash. The Czar tried to retaliate by dumping underpriced potash on the British market, but by 1764 burgeoning English demand and a preference for colonial imports helped the American carbonates to secure the market and retain it until the Revolution.

It was during the pre-revolutionary period that the idea of using pearlash in baking took root and spread. Its high potassium carbonate content made pearlash quite alkaline and a natural counter to the sourness caused by the acid components of a sourdough. It also served an unanticipated function. In reaction with the sourdough acids and with the heat of baking, potassium carbonate decomposed and liberated carbon dioxide gas bubbles. The pearlash not only sweetened the dough, it contributed to its raising as well. This ability of pearlash to create in minutes the leavening gases that required hours from the available yeasts did not go unappreciated.

The popularity of pearlash coincided with and was fueled by several nearly concurrent developments in the United States. The first truly American cookbook, not a European work under an American imprint, was published in 1796 by Amelia Simmons. Her *American Cookery* contained several recipes requiring pearlash. The American housewife had a taste of native recipes. She liked them. The first half of the 19th century did not see many new cookbooks to rival Miss Simmons', but those that did appear devoted much attention to baked goods - bread, rolls, biscuits, cakes, and pastries. Cookies would take a little longer to become popularized by Dutch immigrants.

The home baker had pearlash, and a growing body of instructions on how to use it, plus the ever increasing availability of wheat flour. Oliver Evans pioneered the fine grinding of wheat in America with bolting devices that produced a whiter flour particularly conducive to light and airy, if somewhat reduced in B vitamins, white bread. The country's first automated factory, in fact, was Evans' water driven flour mill built in 1785.

THE SODA ASH REVOLUTION

Although pearlash would remain the premier industrial carbonate in America well into the 19th century, the governments and industries of western Europe recognized that their rapidly expanding need of and dependence upon imported sources of such a basic raw material was politically and economically unwise. There was precious little European woodland left for sacrifice to wood ash, and the only natural alternatives were the limited supplies of crude carbonates produced from the ashes of seaweeds and plants. The situation became sufficiently alarming that the French Academy of Sciences offered a prize in 1783 for the best process for converting common salt to soda ash (sodium carbonate). The prize was claimed in 1791 by Nicolas LeBlanc who secured a patent on his method for reacting salt, sulfuric acid, coal and limestone. With financing from the Duke of Orleans, LeBlanc built a factory to produce soda ash by the process which would thereafter bear his name.

LeBlanc soda ash was produced successfully until 1793 when the French Revolution caused withdrawal of financial support due to the untimely expiration of the Duke. The factory closed and the revolutionary government made the soda ash patent public property. While LeBlanc's factory would not be reactivated until 1808, two years after his suicide, the removal of patent protection encouraged construction of other LeBlanc process soda ash plants. This eventually led to a plentiful supply of sodium carbonate in Europe where it replaced potash and pearlash in industry.

This new availability of soda ash as the basic alkali of European industry redirected attention from the chemistry of potassium carbonate to that of sodium carbonate. By the 1830's, European chemists had experimented with both solution and dry carbonation of sodium carbonate to sodium bicarbonate. The bicarbonate was less alkaline than the carbonate and thus more physiologically compatible. Commercial bicarb begat safe and dependable antacids.

Sodium bicarbonate soon found its way to America under the name saleratus. Saleratus means literally "aerated salt", and was the name coined by the pioneers in bicarbonate chemistry nearly a half century before. In America, this high quality imported saleratus was appreciated for its medical use, but prized as a superior, albeit expensive, alternative to pearlash and American saleratus (potassium bicarbonate) for leavening. Saleratus liberated its carbon dioxide more readily than pearlash, and was less prone to introducing a bitter after-taste if used in excess. The import was likewise of higher purity and offered more dependable results than its American counterpart. It was the market for just such a fine quality sodium bicarbonate which prompted two American entrepeneurs to produce the purer, cheaper saleratus which in time would be found in nearly every home.

RUMFORD'S ROASTER

The last decade of the 18th century gave America and the world the start of a new era in baking with the expanded availability of pearlash, wheat, and cookbooks. Most cooking, however, was done over an open fire, as it had been for centuries. All baking was done in a rudimentary brick oven set into the side of the fireplace.

About 1765, heating stoves with built-in ovens were introduced and became widely available, but these were used strictly as a supplement to the brick oven. Temperature control and standardized baking times were unheard of. The earliest American cookbooks for the most part ignored measurements as well. There were no standardized measuring cups or spoons, and very few kitchens had scales and weights. Cooking and baking were truly a domestic art.

Nevertheless, the seeds of change were being cast. In 1795, the American born Benjamin Thompson, better known as Count Rumford, invented a stove in pursuit of his mission to economically feed Munich's poor. In time, he adapted the size and operation of this stove to produce closed-top wood burning ranges for the home. Heating efficiency was good, and the heat for cooking could be controlled in a limited fashion by manipulation of flues, dampers, and metal plates. The Rumford Roaster enjoyed only brief popularity precisely because of this manipulation, which many found bothersome compared to traditional fireplace cooking. Improvements in design and operation were made by George Bodley in Great Britain, and inventors such as William James, John Conant, and Thomas Woolson in the United States during the first three decades of the 1800's. It was not until the 1870's that familiarity and design improvements made the woodburning iron range a fixture in middle class homes. By then, saleratus was equally well established in home baking, utilizing those stoves to full advantage.

Count Rumford may be long forgotten for his fundamental contribution to baking, but his name lives on in Rumford's Baking Powder, an early stepchild of America's first successful baking soda.

READ'S SALERATUS

The properties of bicarbonates were already known in the latter part of the 18th century since American saleratus was produced as early as 1788 in Massachusetts. Nathan Read of Salem produced saleratus in that year by treating pearlash with the fumes of fermenting molasses. This method probably did not completely convert the pearlash, so that Read's saleratus was likely a blend of both the carbonate and bicarbonate of potassium. His approach, nevertheless, was ingenious, using as a raw material the otherwise wasted carbon dioxide-laden fermentation fumes. Read pioneered the commercial viability of the dry carbonation method. This would serve as the technical foundation of the success and growth of sodium bicarbonate during the second half of the following century.

The technical success of Read's venture is perhaps of lesser importance than why he was interested in saleratus at all. A scholar and inventor, Read had just given up his study of medicine, then largely the study of chemistry, to open an apothecary. There were no industrial uses for bicarbonates at that time, and only limited medical use. His interest was most likely in the production of a superior alternative to pearlash for baking. In those days the lines between general stores and apothecaries were not clearly drawn, so that a new leavener could have been a unique and profitable item for Read's establishment. Whatever his reasons, Read may have been the first American to produce bicarbonate on a commercial scale.

Whether or not Read's saleratus ever found success among his customers is unknown. His attention soon turned away from shopkeeping and toward steam, with the invention of a new boiler, an improved steam engine, and eventually a steam powered boat. If it were not for the derisive response of Congress to his proposition in 1790, he might also have been the first to invent a steam-driven horseless carriage.

BICARB BATTLES

By 1830, adaptations of Read's method made potassium

saleratus readily available from brewers and distillers. This was a natural sideline for the brewers, who had always been a source of yeast for the home baker. They could now offer the faster acting leaven as well. The distillers could likewise profit from the simple method of suspending lump pearlash in perforated wooden boxes in the top of their fermentation vats. The quality of the saleratus so obtained was subject to some inconsistency, however, since impurities were incorporated with the pearlash. The conversion of pearlash to the corresponding saleratus depended on the size of the pearlash lumps and the amount of time they were exposed to the fermentation fumes.

During the 1830's, British sodium saleratus began competing with the American potassium saleratus. Although more expensive than the domestic product, the import offered better quality and consistency. This provided a foothold in the U.S. market, particularly among drug companies and commercial bakers. Recognizing this growing preference for sodium saleratus, the New York distillers, Cogswell & Crane, began manufacturing and selling Soda-Saleratus. Their process was to refine imported soda ash and then treat it in a reverbatory furnace with the carbon dioxide captured from their fermentation vats. Soda-Saleratus enjoyed a brief popularity, but suffered from a fatal flaw. Insufficient time was allowed for the full conversion to bicarbonate. Soda-Saleratus was actually a blend of sodium bicarbonate and unreacted sodium carbonate, and soon succumbed to competition.

One short-lived competitor was Thomas Andrews, a dealer in shelf goods for general stores. He was selling imported English bicarbonate as Excelsior Saleratus. But Andrews had no more lasting success than Cogswell & Crane because of an established specialty chemicals concern, the B.T. Babbitt Co., which brought greater marketing savy to bear.

Benjamin Talbot Babbitt has been characterized as a mechanical genius, with invention the hallmark of his long and uncommonly productive life. His financial success, nevertheless, derived from his flair for chemistry coupled with an intuitive grasp of marketing and promotion in an era when neither were well defined. Babbitt's chemical talents were nurtured solely by lessons he had arranged as a young man in a Utica, New York machine shop. He had convinced his young associates to start work early two days each week so that they could quit one hour sooner for instruction in chemistry. This came by way of a Clinton College professor who Babbitt had induced to travel to Utica on these days to teach the unconventional class.

By the time he arrived in New York City in 1843 at the age of 34, Babbitt was already an expert wheelwright, steam pipe fitter, file maker, blacksmith and general mechanic. He also brought twelve years experience as proprietor of a machine shop where, among more routine work, he had invented one of the country's first mowing machines.

In New York he turned his attention to chemical enterprise and was soon selling sodium carbonate, potash, and saleratus, all of his own manufacture. Babbitt's most significant contribution to the transformation of sodium bicarbonate into a kitchen commodity was not in the fact that he had devised a successful production scheme of his own, but that he broke from the trade norm by offering his saleratus in one pound red paper bags. Instead of the common practice of selling saleratus from open kegs, like flour, sugar and even the milk of that time, shopkeepers kept the distinctive red packages in clear customer view with the other shelf goods. This innovation was supported by Babbitt's gift for promotion. A gift rivaled at the time only by a good friend of his in a somewhat different line of work. The friend was P.T. Barnum.

Babbitt's saleratus claimed the market for a number of years, until replaced by the product that would ultimately popularize sodium bicarbonate throughout the country. Whether Babbitt's saleratus was displaced because of quality or withdrawal of sales support is not known. Babbitt's first love was and always remained mechanics. In fact, nearly all of the apparatus, and many of the procedures used in his factories were reportedly of his own invention. In addition to carbonates and bicarbonates, he produced and sold soap and soap powders. It is in this area that he amassed a substantial fortune.

With his considerable efforts in chemical manufacturing, innovations in soap making ("Babbitt's Best Soap" was immensely popular) and lifelong preoccupation with refining and inventing machines of all types, it is little wonder that his saleratus became just a footnote among his personal and professional accomplishments. Had it been graced with the attention and commitment of another New York entrepeneur, Babbitt's Saleratus might be a household word today.

NATURE'S SALERATUS?

Around the time Babbitt was outmaneuvering Andrews and Cogswell & Crane, pioneers passing the Great Salt Lake in Utah discovered large natural deposits of what they believed was saleratus. This mineral was most likely a mixture of sodium carbonate and sodium bicarbonate not unlike Cogswell & Crane's Soda-Saleratus, and similar to the trona that is a raw material for today's baking soda. The pioneer women collected this mineral, added it to their sourdough bread, and were pleased with the results.

Their name for this mineral indicates that they were well aware of saleratus for baking, but what could have motivated these women to add this salty earth to their bread in the first place? It is unlikely that they knew its chemical composition, or that it might be a natural alternative to pearlash or manufactured saleratus.

More likely it was initially substituted for what it appeared to be - salt. Salt would be added to sourdough simply for flavor. Or it is possible that it was added to the type of sourdough used for making salt-rising bread. The starter for this type of bread is made from a mixture of water, cornmeal, sugar and salt. The subsequent fermentation of added flour and milk produces leavening, and a characteristically disagreeable odor. Despite the term salt-rising, only a small amount of salt was actually used, and it did not even contribute to the raising of the dough. Salt-rising is thought a corruption of the original description of this dough as self-rising.

Even though they produce excellent and distinctively flavored breads, salt-rising doughs are rarely prepared today because they are very finicky, and very smelly. They require fermentation at a relatively high temperature for about twelve hours. As often as not these days they just do not raise. The secret to salt-rising dough is, according to some, the use of fresh ground or unprocessed cornmeal and raw milk, neither of which is readily available any longer. The westward pioneers in the first half of the 19th century, however, would have had both at hand. Corn was the most common and widely used grain of the time, and raw milk was as close as the family's goat or cow. An alternative to raw milk that is used today, and certainly would have been a natural alternative then, was potato water. This produced a still fouler smelling dough. Even if a family did not bring a milking animal on its migration, potatoes would have been a staple of their larder. It is not difficult to believe that daytime temperatures inside a covered wagon on the Great Salt Lake Desert would be sufficiently high to aid fermentation.

Those pioneer cooks probably added this salty mineral to a salt-rising dough and then observed that as the milk soured, the dough rose higher and more quickly than expected, as if it were saleratus rather than salt that had been added. A little trial and error, and the conclusion that this was a natural form of saleratus would be reasonable.

The accessibility and apparently endless supply of this mineral saleratus undoubtedly earned it some measure of local popularity. It was never to seriously compete with manufactured saleratus, however, because of lack of suitable haulage out of the Utah frontier, lack of purity for food use, and because an enterprising doctor figured out how to make pure and cheap sodium bicarbonate, while his brother-in-law recognized its potential for consumer use.

THE DETERMINED DOCTOR

While most of settled America was discovering the advantages of saleratus over pearlash, and well before New York consumers witnessed the Babbitt Co.'s temporary victory in the saleratus wars, Dr. Austin Church, a Connecticut native and graduate of Yale, was experimenting with the synthesis of sodium bicarbonate. On the basis of work begun in his kitchen in Ithaca, New York, Dr. Church decided to trade his medical practice for the commercial production of saleratus. In 1834 he uprooted his wife and children and moved to Rochester. The possible reasons for his decision to abandon medicine, and his choice of Rochester are reflections of his time and possibly of his motivation.

In that era, and for most of the 19th century, the practice of medicine was not the gainful and highly regarded profession it is today. A doctor's patented approach to most maladies was either bleeding the patient, dosing with calomel (a toxic mercury compound), or both. Although by the 1830's bloodletting was generally performed in the modern fashion, with a lance rather than leeches, results were no more favorable. Despite their Hippocratic mandate to "Do no harm," many doctors of this time were generally mistrusted, if not downright feared, and in fact were more likely to deliver the seriously ill to their reward than to good health.

During the first half of the 19th century, both chemistry and medicine were in the process of dissociating themselves from their common heritage - alchemy. Although the healing arts lagged the science in this effort, it was formal medical training that provided the vehicle for the development of the study of chemistry. In the U.S., formal instruction in chemistry was first introduced in the curricula of medical schools. From colonial times until the latter 1800's, when American manufacturing grew to truly industrial scale, it was often physicians, those with training in chemistry and conversant with the chemical literature of the time, who would dabble in chemical enterprises. In Dr. Church's time, it was no small irony that medical schools were elevating the science of chemistry above the potions of alchemy, while their graduates were still mired in the practices of the Middle Ages.

It is not surprising that Dr. Church saw greater opportunity, and financial security, in the commercial manufacture of saleratus than in pursuing a small town medical practice. His choice of Rochester was undoubtedly equally well reasoned. Following the opening of the Rochester and Lockport section of the Erie Canal in 1823, Rochester's proximity to the wheat fields of the Genessee Valley had propelled it to the status of leading flour milling center of the United States. When the Church family arrived in 1834, Rochester had just recently received its city charter, Genessee Valley flour had earned worldwide fame, and the Rochester mills were turning out more than 300,000 barrels per year.

Dr. Church's intent was presumably to produce saleratus in bulk for sale to the flour mills' far flung customers. Rochester's population of 12,000 would have been insufficient to sustain volume output of household saleratus for Dr. Church's factory, and the concept of self-rising flour was still more than a decade and a half in the future. He may have pursued the bulk market by persuading the millers to include his saleratus on their price lists as a convenience to their customers. He also may have written directly to prospects on the basis of customer lists supplied by the millers.

The process Dr. Church perfected in his Rochester factory was to first take imported LeBlanc process soda ash and meticulously purify it. The refined sodium carbonate was then spread thinly over canvas covered wooden frames stacked in a sealed room. For three weeks, this room was filled with hot gases containing carbon dioxide from coal fired ovens. By this dry carbonation method, the purified sodium carbonate was entirely converted to food grade sodium bicarbonate.

The bulk saleratus business allowed the Church family a comfortable existence, but apparently not an especially prosperous one. In 1842, they moved to Oswego, ostensibly to provide the doctor a steadier income from the practice of medicine. Residency here was to be short lived, however, thanks to Dr. Church's brother-in-law, John Dwight, a young entrepeneur with a vision for saleratus. In 1846, the Church family moved once again, this time to New York City.

DWIGHT'S SALERATUS

Undoubtedly familiar with the fortunes of his sister's family in Rochester, and the subsequent move to Oswego, John Dwight envisioned a market for sodium bicarbonate that was not obvious to Austin Church. He realized that the key to success, in addition to selling in bulk to commercial bakers and drug companies, was to build a consumer franchise by selling saleratus in packages through the retail trade. Whether he was unaware of the success of Babbitt's saleratus, or encouraged by it, remains unknown. He could appreciate, nevertheless, how producing the product domestically would provide a price advantage over the imports, the quality of which he was convinced his brother-in-law's product could match or exceed.

By 1846, New York was already the leading port of the nation, the only seaport with access, via the Erie Canal, to the Great Lakes region. This meant that shipping costs for soda ash from England and distribution costs for finished bicarbonate would be very low. As the young country's largest city, New York also offered a large potential market for household use of saleratus - a potential that the Babbitt company was already exploiting. The Church family from Oswego, and the Dwight family from South Hadley, Massachusetts, converged on New York City in 1846 to found John Dwight & Company. Dr. Church assumed responsibility for manufacturing, and John Dwight for sales. In that year the distinctively red labeled "Dwight's Saleratus", in bags of one pound or less, was first offered by Dwight to New York's storekeepers.

Within a few years, Dwight's Saleratus capitalized on its claims of superior quality and value. It captured the New York market, and started expanding into every inhabited part of the country. Competition, especially in rural areas, was mainly the well established imported saleratus sold loose in kegs. But the distinctive red-wrapped bags of Dwight's Saleratus inevitably became the baker's choice. By 1850, the American housewife could purchase domestically produced saleratus from the general store for 4¢/lb.; quite an improvement over the $1.25/lb. her mother had paid for the import in 1820.

The 1850's brought financial stability to Dwight & Co., along with a force of salesmen to promote Dwight's Saleratus in every town or settlement large enough to boast a general store. Saleratus was fast becoming a kitchen necessity. Success, of course, bred new competition as other manufacturers saw there was money to be made in tapping this new market for low cost, high quality domestic bicarbonate. The 1860's witnessed new brands from small firms, like Philadelphia's Burgin & Sons, to the mighty Pennsylvania Salt Manufacturing Company. The most effective competition to emerge from the 1860's, however, was from Dr. Austin Church.

ARM & HAMMER

In 1865, the 66 year old Dr. Church decided to retire from John Dwight & Company. He had wanted to start his two sons in the business. This was also John Dwight's intention for one of his sons. A major independent investor in the company strenuously objected, however, effectively barring entry of the second generation. Rather than creating controversy within the company, Dr. Church chose to retire. Two years later he helped his two sons, James and Elihu Church, both successful businessmen in their own right, to found Church & Company. Recognizing there was sufficient need in the rapidly expanding U.S. to accommodate a competitor with quality equal to Dwight's Saleratus, they constructed a factory in Greenpoint, Brooklyn devoted to sodium bicarbonate.

James had been a partner in the Vulcan Spice Mills, a Brooklyn mustard and spice business, from which he brought the Arm & Hammer logo. This symbol represented the arm of Vulcan, mythological god of fire and metalworking, with hammer raised. While perhaps better suited to the spice trade, this trademark was distinctively recognizable and soon intimately associated with what became the country's best selling bicarb. Dwight's Saleratus and Arm & Hammer Bicarbonate of Soda became the dominant rivals in the chemical leavening business, but the rivalry was friendly and mutually beneficial.

IN-LAWS & LABELS

As both companies strove to expand their business, they

established and expanded the nationwide market for their products. Each helped establish sodium bicarbonate as a household necessity, and each benefited. That the competition was friendly is demonstrated by John Dwight's first attempt to improve his product's brand recognition. In 1870, he commissioned Elihu Church, an accomplished artist and co-owner of his chief competitor, to design an eye catching label for Dwight's Saleratus. Church did such an effective job that the label, depicting a typical rural kitchen scene of the period, was admired by customers, and copied with only slight modification by the Pennsylvania Salt Manufacturing Co. for its saleratus. Despite passage of the federal Registered Trademark Act in 1870, Dwight had little recourse in challenging the plagiarizing firm, which was considerably larger than his and better able to commit resources to litigation.

Dwight dropped the label and shortly replaced it with one featuring the bovine Lady Maud, a cow of no small fame. Lady Maud, a pedigreed Jersey, was the toast of the 1876 Philadelphia Centennial Exposition. Dwight secured exclusive rights to her likeness, and Dwight's Saleratus soon became known as the soda with the cow on the package. Taking the cue from his customers, Dwight rechristened his product "Dwight's Soda, Cow Brand." Lady Maud and Cow Brand would endure well into the 20th century.

The strength of family over business would again be demonstrated some two decades later when in 1891 a fire destroyed the Greenpoint plant of Church & Company. Once their salvaged inventory sold out, and until the plant was rebuilt, John Dwight & Co. helped keep them supplied. It would take until 1896, however, for the descendants of John Dwight and Austin Church to consolidate their interests.

In the fifty years following the two families' move to New York, sodium bicarbonate became as common a household item as sugar, flour, or salt. Those five decades witnessed as well the unique confluence of social, religious, and political events in the rapidly expanding United States that sodium bicarbonate would both contribute to and exploit. This ensured its success in the marketplace, and laid the foundation for its status as an American folk phenomenon.

AN AMERICAN TALE

An appreciation of the uniquely American rise of baking soda is best prefaced with why sodium bicarbonate never gained similar culinary status in Europe, particularly Britain. Prior to Babbitt's and Dwight's products, expensive English imports were the main source in America. The same year that John Dwight started his rounds of the New York City shopkeepers, the first commercial baking powder, Millers, appeared in England. This was some nine years before the first American baking powder was marketed by Preston & Merrill of Boston. In both countries baking powder, a mixture of baking soda and cream of tartar, was met with more than a little skepticism by consumers who were unconvinced of the purity, dependability or need of such a product. In the U.S., saleratus was already a familiar and available commodity at the general store, so housewives were more inclined to simply make use of it with sour milk or with cream of tartar. In Britain, however, sodium bicarbonate was an expensive apothecary item.

The British baking powder manufacturers countered mistrust of their product by taking advantage of an almost concurrent and seemingly competitive culinary advance. At that time, so-called German or compressed yeast, similar to today's yeast cake, was gaining popularity. Although not dry, it was commonly referred to as dried yeast. Once the baking powder producers realized their product would not be an easy sell, they started a long, concerted, and shameless campaign of advertising it as yeast powder, yeast substitute, or dried yeast. They even used brand names calculated to help the consumer confuse baking powder with yeast. From the 1860's onward, baking powders and then self-rising flours became firmly established for household baking in Britain. Bicarbonate of soda remained a fairly obscure ingredient available at relatively high cost only from the apothecary, a situation that for the most part still exists.

American baking powder manufacturers did not have the temerity, or well developed advertising outlets at first, to take similar advantage of the commercial introduction of yeast cake in this country in 1868. Instead of riding its coattails, legitimately or not, baking powder suffered from a continuing concern over purity and dependability, as well as competition from the well accepted saleratus. This turned out to be a win-win situation for both the Dwight and Church companies. They had secured the dominant position in the consumer market for saleratus, based largely on product quality and customer satisfaction, but they supported their main mission with bulk sales. Their established positions as producers of high quality sodium bicarbonate helped establish them as valued suppliers to the struggling baking powder industry.

This position would eventually bear fruit when baking powders became well accepted among both home and commercial bakers. The antecedents of some of today's largest baking companies were also early customers of Dwight and of Church. Bulk customers included the American Biscuit and Manufacturing Co., the New York Biscuit Co., and the U.S. Baking Co., all three of which would form the National Biscuit Co. (Nabisco), as well as the Loose Wiles Biscuit Co., which became the Sunshine Biscuit Company.

READING, WRITING AND RECIPES

By 1850, the tax-supported public school system had been established in the United States, approximately 50 years ahead of a similar development in Great Britain. The rapidly expanding U.S. literacy was exploited by the bicarbonate producers to reinforce brand recognition, loyalty, and usage. Recipes compiled and tested by Mrs. Dwight were supplied free with each package of Dwight's Saleratus. Beginning in 1860, recipe booklets were distributed using mass mailings based on lists obtained from postmasters, and later compiled from telephone books.

Because of its wide availability in general stores, saleratus was placed in countless households where innovative men and women found other uses for this cheap and versatile chemical. For example, one of the first non-food uses of sodium bicarbonate was as a tooth powder. Dental hygiene, when it was practiced at all, was little more sophisticated than cleaning teeth with salt or ground oyster shell. While salt could offer some bactericidal properties and relatively mild abrasivity, it must have been quite uncomfortable on the ravaged gums that were a common result of the generally poor state of dentition at the time. A fine saleratus powder that could clean teeth and actually sooth rather than irritate diseased gums must have quickly become popular. As consumers related the new uses they had discovered, the producers were quick to include this information along with recipes in promotional flyers.

The growth of American literacy in the second half of the 19th century naturally prompted the proliferation of literature. It bred that bastion of U.S. publishing as well - the cookbook. In some cases there were surprising common denominators. As Lady Maria Clutterbuck, Mrs. Charles Dickens published *What Shall We Have For Dinner*, while in 1865, *House and Home Papers* was published by Harriet Beecher Stowe under the pseudonym of Christopher Crowfield. In 1879, bicarbonate of soda was so well established that it was the recommended leavener in a number of baked goods recipes in Miss T.S. Shute's *The American Housewife* - not an especially remarkable occurrence it would seem, except that this book had been sponsored by a baking powder company.

With the help of the two major bicarbonate producers, and the proliferation of cookbooks, American housewives were gaining an appreciation of the merits of chemical leavening. They used soda with sour milk or cream of tartar for batters and quick breads, where the competition was not yeast but time and muscle. Anything that would cut down on the labor involved in physically beating air into batters was certainly welcomed. Bicarbonate of soda may still have been added to sourdough breads, but any attempts to replace yeast in other raised breads were eventually abandoned. Americans had developed a fondness for the taste of yeast-leavened bread and there was little point in fighting it.

This, nevertheless, was not a wholly uncontested victory for yeast cake. It had to contend with societal influences in America that it escaped in other countries, lending advantage to baking soda as the only viable alternative. Yeast earned its place in bread but relinquished whatever tenuous hold it may have had in most other baked goods.

MOVERS AND SHAKERS

The U.S. health food movement which began early in the 1800's played a major role in securing the future of baking soda. This movement was motivated by what was seen as a general malaise among American urbanites. The largely sedentary city folk were accustomed to breakfasts of steak and pie, and greasy foods at nearly every meal. These frequently dyspeptic citizens were primed for new ideas and whatever convenient cure-all that might come their way. Reform, both social and religious, became a cause celebre.

As one of the first groups to establish communities dedicated to regular and simple living habits, the Shakers advocated whole grain flours in baking and greater use of vegetables and fruits. Much attention, of course, was given to the proper baking of bread.

Roller mills were gaining in popularity at that time for the whiter, although somewhat vitamin deficient, wheat flour they produced. The roller mill squeezed the grain such that the endosperm popped out of its coating, leaving the wheat germ behind to be sieved off with the bran. The germ took with it the oils that had given "white" flour a characteristically yellow hue and had let the flour become rancid in just a few weeks. Roller milled flour was whiter and would last longer. This was seen as an unquestionable benefit by everyone from miller and baker, to grocer and customer, who equated the whiteness of bread with quality and purity. Even the urban poor could have the whitest white bread, unaware that the cost was loss of the nutrients from the wheat germ - a loss that could be ill afforded by people who used bread as the mainstay of their diet.

While the populace as a whole welcomed whiter flours and breads, the Shakers saw them as a corruption and railed against millers who removed the germ from the wheat. They were among the first to insist on the entire wheat kernel being ground for flour.

The Shaker advocacy of whole wheat flour reached Sylvester Graham, a young Connecticut zealot looking for a cause. Following expulsion from Amherst College and a nervous breakdown, Graham had become a Presbyterian preacher, vegetarian, temperance lecturer, self-proclaimed diet expert, and self-styled doctor of medicine. For two decades before the Civil War, he proselytized on health and moral grounds against refined white flour and white bread. He advocated only coarsely ground whole wheat flour for bread, which was to be eaten slightly stale. Graham had no knowledge of the nutrients lost from white flour, and was likely reacting on a more visceral level. Whole wheat bread does have a more distinctive taste than white. Of probably greater moment, however, is that it promotes bowel regularity from bran's laxative effect. This was an obsession which Graham nearly institutionalized for health food faddists in succeeding generations - a legacy rivaled only by the ubiquitous brown crackers still bearing his name.

Gastrointestinal difficulties were so common that his eloquent teachings fell on fertile ground. Grahamite societies formed and grocery stores appeared that specialized in items recommended by the master. Sylvester Graham chose not to campaign categorically against yeast-leavened bread, although he ironically considered the nutritive brewer's yeast a poison, understandable from a temperance advocate, and maintained that the overfermentation that produced sourdough was a depredation. The use of "sweet" domestic yeast was allowed, although this may have been by default and a concession to Graham's pragmatic side. Whole wheat bread made from sourdough was obviously unthinkable and other alternatives must have been recognized as ranging from less palatable to barely digestible. If people were going to benefit from his whole wheat bread, it would have to have at least a basic culinary appeal. Baking soda's place may have found some direction in Graham's admission that sodium bicarbonate and tartaric acid were handy for making pancakes.

The influence of food faddists from Graham onward can perhaps be measured more by their disciples than by their sometimes bizarre disciplines. The subtle promulgation of ideas by the advocates of one newly popular concept or another is often what turns quackery into conventional wisdom. Graham's followers included breakfast cereal moguls John and Will Kellogg, Oberlin College founders John J. Shipherd and Philo Penfield Stewart, Mormon Church founder Joseph Smith, and Fruitlands Commune founder Bronson Alcott (father of Louisa

May); Horace Greely and Thomas Edison were believers, if not radical adherents.

EBEN'S BETTER LEAVEN

Into this growing American grassroots phenomenon came saleratus, and Louis Pasteur. In 1857, Dr. Pasteur discovered that yeast is composed of microorganisms whose activity cause fermentation. The health food adherents did not accept this in the spirit of enlightenment with which it was intended. As far as they were concerned, wheat flours and breads were not only being debased in the cause of whiteness, they were being infused with microorganisms in the act of leavening as well. The official scientific imprimatur came in 1861 via Harvard's Rumford (in honor of the Count) Professor of Applied Science, Eben Horsford. In his treatise on bread making, he compared the yeast organism to poisonous molds and quoted several learned colleagues on the dangers of microbes. He suggested a mixture of sodium bicarbonate and dry phosphate of lime (monocalcium phosphate). This particular baking powder formula was deemed superior because its residues, lime and sodium phosphate, are found in the human body and were presumed harmless.

Professor Horsford had not come to this position from an entirely unbiased point of view. In 1854 he had been hired as a consultant by a manufacturer of textile chemicals in Rhode Island. Two years later this developed into an informal manufacturing partnership. Around this time, Horsford also started working in his Cambridge laboratory on an idea that would result in America's first truly domestic baking powder.

By the 1850's, cream of tartar had largely replaced sour milk in the East as the acid adjunct to sodium bicarbonate for leavening. The urban housewife routinely stocked separate supplies of saleratus and cream of tartar, or purchased "baking powder", a single container holding separate packages of saleratus and cream of tartar.

Cream of tartar, a by-product of wine production, was available primarily from Italy, and from France. Since Italy's political difficulties with Austria were making the supply and price of cream of tartar rather erratic, Horsford conceived the notion that an acid salt of phosphoric acid should be a suitable alternative and would return to the flour the phosphate lost in milling. To make the acid phosphate, Horsford and his partner, George Wilson, had to develop a commercial process for producing phosphoric acid. This they did based on the raw materials then available - bones, in endless supply from slaughterhouses, and spent bone black from sugar refining.

By 1859, the newly incorporated Rumford Chemical Works was producing the monocalcium phosphate, patented as "pulverulent phosphoric acid", which would release the carbon dioxide from the bicarbonate. One of Horsford's first customers was Preston & Merrill, the country's first baking powder producer, which was quick to recognize the advantages of the monocalcium phosphate over the cream of tartar it had been using.

"Horsford's Cream of Tartar Substitute" was already on the market when the professor was inveighing against yeast leavening. This apparently self-serving position against yeast did not prevent the Rumford Chemical Works from offering "Rumford's Yeast Powder" in 1864. This was a blend of sodium bicarbonate and monocalcium phosphate sealed in a glass jar to prevent chemical reaction before use. Four years before Fleischman & Co. of Cincinnatti introduced the first American compressed yeast, Rumford Chemical came to the same conclusion as its British counterparts. There could be economic advantage in blurring the lines between baking powder and yeast.

Horsford had meanwhile retired from Harvard in 1863 to devote himself to his private laboratory and the exploration of food uses of monocalcium phosphate. He recognized the potential for a stable mixture of soda and his acid if it could be conveniently packaged in a metal can instead of a fragile glass bottle. He discovered that dry starch added to the mixture would absorb any airborne moisture that would otherwise cause the bicarbonate and phosphate powders to react. As a result, Eben Horsford's most enduring contribution to baking was introduced in 1869, in metal cans. Inside each can, the sodium bicarbonate component was from Dr. Church's process. Outside each can was the silhouette of Count Rumford - fitting since the descendants of his Rumford Roaster have helped keep Rumford Baking Powder unchanged and in demand ever since.

RUTT'S BETTER IDEA

Horsford, in his 1861 treatise, also pointed out that a handy self-rising flour could be made by mixing the sodium bicarbonate and phosphate of lime with flour. He, in fact, patented such a composition in 1864. This would make a dough that could be mixed and ready for baking within minutes. The idea for a self-rising flour actually preceded Horsford by about 10 years, but his suggestion would not see successful commercialization in the U.S. until 1889, when Chris Rutt, a St. Joseph, Missouri newspaperman and ardent pancake aficionado, decided there must be an alternative to mixing pancakes from scratch every morning. He put a blend of flour, bicarbonate of soda, monocalcium phosphate and salt in a plain paper bag and sold it to local grocers. Sales were not encouraging.

Confident of the quality of his product, Rutt realized that it would need better packaging to sell. Inspiration soon came at a local vaudeville show. A featured number was "Aunt Jemima" sung by a pair of blackface minstrels, one of whom was dressed as a traditional Southern cook in apron and red bandana. Rutt borrowed the song title and the image of Southern hospitality conveyed by a "mammy" for his pancake package. Sales grew enough to convince the Davis Milling Co. to buy out Rutt's interests in the product. They decided to promote Aunt Jemima Pancake Mix at the 1893 Chicago World's Fair, introducing a gimmick that advertisers have embraced ever since. They searched among Chicago's domestics until they found an affable black cook named Nancy Green to serve as the personification of Aunt Jemima. Nancy Green served the fair's visitors more than one million pancakes, and toured the country as Aunt Jemima until her death in 1923.

OPENED MARKETS

Before branded goods like Arm & Hammer and Cow Brand could be promoted and effectively distributed, there had to be a reliable and economical transportation system to move them. The east and west coasts of the U.S. were united when the Union Pacific and Central Pacific railroads were joined with a symbolic gold spike on May 10, 1869. This event was of special significance to artist and businessman Elihu Church. The businessman saw the entire country opened to his Arm & Hammer Bicarbonate of Soda. The artist undoubtedly reflected upon the period following his Civil War service when he was the official artist of the Union Pacific as it laid track toward that historic day.

With the railroads united, all major markets became accessible. Transcontinental transportation was now available, but expensive. It was the profit-inspired strategy of the railroads, assisted by the federal government, that made widespread distribution of packaged goods economical, while not incidentally transforming the Central Plains into America's breadbasket.

The uniting of East and West was a singular technological

achievement, but the railroads recognized that it would not be a profitable one with so much of the country empty. The passengers and freight from west of the Rockies and east of the Mississippi had to subsidize the operation of the trains through the empty half of the cross country trip which lay between. To stay in business, the railroads would have to set their prices so high that they couldn't attract enough business to survive. Their solution was simple and based on the thousands of workers they had brought to the interior of the country to build the railroad itself. They encouraged these people, many of whom were immigrants, to settle in the territories they had opened, instead of returning home.

The federal government was willing to provide free land to citizen homesteaders, who in most cases had the money to start a new life because there had been no place to spend their railroad wages in the barren land. Since many of the railworkers were foreigners and ineligible for free homesteading land, the railroads sold them land on credit out of the extensive holdings the government had granted to encourage expansion.

The new settlers converted the "wastelands" of the Central Plains into one of the world's richest granaries, tilling 400 million acres of virgin soil between 1860 and 1900. The railroads obliged, as planned, by providing bulk transportation of these grains throughout the country and to the major ports for exportation to foreign markets. The transportation of grain, the people who raised and milled it, and the livestock that was fattened on it solidified the strength and the future of the railroads. It also opened up to this large and still new country vast untapped markets for consumer goods - markets the merchandising entrepeneurs were ready to exploit. Once again, the focus on health and hygiene, both religiously and scientifically inspired, was directed toward profit, the ultimate motivation.

CLOSED CONTAINERS

Until the latter 1800's, food and grocery items were generally transported and sold in bulk. Grocers would typically display sugar, flour, saleratus, milk, cheese and butter in quantity and uncovered. Even after the characterization of bacteria and the efficiency with which flies and rodents disseminate them, packaged goods were slow to catch on. But gradually they did. Packaging was more hygenic for the customer, and also more profitable for the producer because it helped protect perishables from damage and spoilage, while facilitating transport and storage. Right from the start, John Dwight supplied his saleratus for the retail trade in packages, rather than in bulk.

The slow but inexorable movement from bulk to branded goods followed the progress in packaging technology. The year 1852 marked Francis Wolle's patenting of the first paper bag making machine, moving this most fundamental packaging form from hand craft to industry. His Union Paper Bag Machine Company quickly secured 90% of the market. Each succeeding decade saw additional major advances. The 1860's brought the square-bottom bag, courtesy of Luther Childs Crowell; the 1870's, new techniques for printing on metal, enabling decorated tins; the 1880's, machine-produced folding cardboard cartons, the first automatic canning lines and the now standard "self-opening" bags of Charles Stillwell. These were pleated on the sides to fold flat for storage but open by the simple flick of a clerk's wrist.

Both the Dwight and Church companies took advantage of American packaging innovations, further solidifying their position in America's stores and homes. They also made contributions of their own. In the early 1880's, James McCrodden invented an automatic filling machine for Dwight & Co. which greatly improved the productivity and the already high standards of hygiene under which Cow Brand was packaged. Within a few years, Albert Stearns, superintendent of the Church & Co. plant, invented a package wrapping machine that increased output of Arm & Hammer from 1000 to 15,000 packages per day.

COMMERCE, AMERICAN STYLE

The success of baking soda in carving a secure consumer niche was due in no small part to the manner in which it worked within and around America's changing systems of trade. In the mid-1800's, the American retail trade embraced a spectrum of sophistication, dealing as it did with everything from the urban East to the primitive frontier towns. For the country as a whole, the general flow of goods was from manufacturer, to wholesaler, to shopkeeper. Until the 1870's, there was little retail specialization, with most goods available through the general store. Manufacturers commonly sold their output to wholesalers, who in turn would service thousands of individual stores. The dominant force in this scheme was the wholesalers.

Wholesalers exerted considerable leverage with the manufacturers because they usually offered the most cost-effective means of distribution. Most producers could not consider the expense of mounting a national or even regional sales force, but needed a reasonably steady outlet for their output. The wholesalers would purchase from several manufacturers so their salesmen could offer a broad line of items to the retail merchants. The downside for the manufacturers was that the wholesalers often handled competitive goods and used this leverage to exact the lowest possible prices. They also preferentially promoted those items which afforded them the best profit. In time it even became common for the wholesalers to own their own factories and further dominate profitable markets. The upside for the producers was that the network of wholesalers' salesmen, covering everywhere from big cities to one horse towns, expanded the market for their manufactured goods.

The wholesalers likewise exerted control over their customers, the shopkeepers. Much trade in general stores and, into the early 20th century, in grocery stores was done "on the book." Customers bought on credit, settling with the store owner once or twice a month as a paycheck was received. Payment came only once a year in some rural areas where most income was earned, and bills paid, only when the crops were sold. Just as the store owners became de facto lenders to their customers, the wholesalers became the financial underpinnings of much of the retail trade. Thousands of small retailers existed on their ability to maintain liberal credit terms with their wholesalers.

The early conversion of grocery items from bulk to packages may have been instigated by concern over hygiene, damage, or spoilage, all of which worked mainly to the detriment of wholesaler and retailer. Labeling those packages invited conflict among all members of the distribution chain. Bulk items, if marked at all, would as often bear the mark of the wholesaler as of the manufacturer. Consumers had no means to know, and for the most part no interest in knowing, who produced the sugar or flour or saleratus their merchant scooped from the barrel. If there was a complaint about quality, it was the merchant's problem and responsibility to correct.

As packaged goods were introduced, the courting of consumer preference naturally followed. The flour or sugar or saleratus was elevated from the keg on the floor, often behind the counter where it was not seen anyway, to the packages in plain sight on the shelves behind the clerk. Sight recognition assumed no small significance since most stores were full service, and would remain so into the early 20th century. The customer would either have to point out what was wanted, or request it by name or package description. The value of a visually distinctive package became obvious.

The wholesalers naturally preferred the packaged goods they distributed to bear their name. This way they could foster brand loyalty among consumers, but still control the sources and prices of the products that filled their packages. The store owners preferred to put their own mark on packaged goods, since they were primarily interested in developing consumer loyalty to their stores, not to particular goods. Since they had to personally vouch for quality and live by whatever profits they could earn, they wanted a firmer hand in customer buying habits. Manufacturers likewise saw the advantages of a more direct link with the ultimate purchasers by branding their own goods, but were probably motivated more by the desire to maintain some measure of control over pricing and demand for their products. The tradeoff was their direct accountability for quality.

Not surprisingly, the store owners, individually without clout, soon abandoned any hope of having their own brands placed on packages. Wholesalers and producers continued jockeying for position on the issue, ultimately invading each other's turf, and the retailers'. By the end of the century, the retail distribution system was disorganized at best, chaotic at worst. As manufacturers grew, those that had the financial muscle established their own brands and their own lines of distribution. This allowed them to better reconcile output with demand and gave them control over pricing and profitability. A common attitude was that once they had created brand loyalty for their goods, wholesalers would subordinate their own preferences to simply make money by responding to producer-cultivated consumer demand. Many manufacturers eventually relied on combinations of direct salesmen, their own warehouses, wholesalers, and independent middlemen. Some companies even established their own retail operations, selling door-to-door, through the mail, or in their own retail stores. Others took advantage of their established distribution systems to serve as wholesalers for other manufacturers.

Although the largest retailers would eventually cross into wholesaling and manufacturing, most were caught in the middle of this power struggle engendered by the packaging and branding of goods. Well into the late 1800's some grocery commodities like flour and bicarbonate of soda were still even offered in bulk because many storekeepers felt that this allowed them the best profit. Meanwhile, their customers were showing a distinct preference for packaged and branded goods because this provided added reliability in obtaining the level of quality they desired.

Wholesalers generally offered merchants better discounts on their "private label" brands than the manufacturers could or would. This went a long way in the grocery trade toward convincing retailers to stock and promote these substitutes for the "name" or national brands. The manufacturers realized that they were at a disadvantage in this scenario since the store owners would naturally sell the goods that maximized their profit. These merchants also maintained considerable influence on the buying decisions of their customers in these full service days. This made it easy for the storekeeper to steer customers to the most profitable brands. The manufacturers countered this by going directly to the root of the problem - the customer. Advertising as we know it was born.

Since colonial times, newspapers and magazines had published paid commercial messages, but these were usually in special sections of closely packed small ads, much like today's classifieds. Their main function was to let potential customers know that the goods were available. Starting in the 1870's, magazines like *Harpers*, *Scribners*, and in the 1880's the newly published *Ladies Home Journal*, helped revolutionize advertising. They made available space for large, well designed ads at reasonable rates. Advertising revenue helped turn mass-circulation magazines and major newspapers into advertising media. Manufacturers exploited this means to communicate directly with and influence consumers in favor of their name brands. This eventually diminished the influence of the shopkeeper and his ability to successfully push more profitable substitute brands. To further pressure the independent grocer in this dawning age of advertising came an entirely new system of distribution and promotion.

The mass merchandising revolution was pioneered by George F. Gilman and George Huntington Hartford when in 1859 they opened a little store in New York City to sell tea. America was then a great tea drinking country, and Hartford had conceived a method to serve its need efficiently and profitably. Tea had traditionally been purchased as a necessary luxury, so shopkeepers used it as a high margin item to offset low or no profit necessities like flour and milk. Hartford's innovation was to buy as close to the Asian source as possible, eliminating the markup of middlemen, and to buy in enormous quantities to secure the best price. In effect, Gilman and Hartford became their own wholesaler. The considerable savings they enjoyed were passed on to their customers, allowing them to greatly underprice all competition. They were rewarded in short order with a thriving business and the ire of shopkeepers bound to the conventional distribution system.

In 1861, Gilman christened the enterprise the Great American Tea Company, reflecting more his vision for its growth than its actual size. By 1865, the company was operating the largest tea store in the world, plus five branch stores, all in New York City. It was time to expand and earn its name.

The two entrepreneurs realized that growth could be had with little competition, but that establishing a succession of retail stores would be time and capital consuming. Instead of concentrating solely on retail expansion, they instituted a mail order plan which cast them as wholesalers as well. This plan encouraged groups of merchants and individuals to form tea-buying "clubs." These clubs could buy tea at a deep discount, with the organizer of each receiving complimentary quantities. Members were thereby given incentive to buy, and to organize their own clubs. This ancestor of multilevel marketing was hugely successful and helped finance the proliferation of the neighborhood tea stores. Sales were supported by a complementary blend of advertising, gift premiums and the first use of trading stamps, which could be redeemed for a variety of household items.

In 1869, the company celebrated the joining of East and West by rail, and its own prosperity, by changing its name to the Great Atlantic & Pacific Tea Company. The retail stores, the A&P as they and the company came to be called, were concentrated in urban neighborhoods convenient to their customers. To serve the large but disseminated rural populations, A&P established in the 1870s a network of rural wagon routes under the original Great American Tea Company name. This rural home delivery business soon incorporated a broad line of condiments and household items. Soon after, A&P added coffee to its stores and became increasingly attracted to the idea of expanding its offerings along the lines of its rural subsidiary. It took until the 1890's, however, for A&P, then numbering more than 100 stores east of the Mississippi, to make the first move in the evolution from tea shops to grocery stores.

This transformation was significant in sidestepping the conventional grocery marketing of the time. Success in high volume/low margin selling of tea and coffee without benefit of wholesalers convinced the company to apply the same approach to most other grocery items. As wholesalers and name brand manufacturers battled in the grocery stores, A&P went a step beyond just avoiding middlemen. The company decided it could provide the highest quality at the best price by offering its own brands wherever possible. By slowly integrating their own manufacturing and wholesaling, A&P developed a new way to feed America.

At the turn of the century, when advertising was prompting the general preference among consumers for name brands, the growing A&P chain set off on an entirely different course toward dominance in grocery retailing. It carried some name brands, bought directly from the manufacturers, but it stressed the value of its store brands. A&P advertising promoted value over brand names.

Through the first dozen years of the 20th century inflation in America seriously impacted the cost of living in general and the price of food in particular. As A&P grew to 400 stores during this period, its heavy use of premiums and trading stamps as incentives threatened its ability to maintain the lowest price structure in retailing. In 1912, the company experimented with a new type of food market which seemed better able to employ the low price philosophy. The Economy Store was intentionally established around the corner from a large and successful A&P in Jersey City. The new store was small, nondescript and designed to operate at minimal expense. There was no advertising, no delivery, no telephone orders, no premiums, no trading stamps and no advertising. The store offered only low prices and a single clerk.

Within six months the Economy Store forced the nearby A&P out of business. The company had a new direction. Over the next four years, A&P opened 7500 new stores using the economy format, and closed more than half of these as the weakest were weeded out. As the retail operation mushroomed, the cost of goods was controlled by the gradual increase in self-manufactured store brands plus the growing leverage exerted on the remaining private label suppliers of their store brands. As the country's single largest food retailer, A&P assumed the negotiating edge in exacting the best prices from its vendors. Manufacturing its own goods, or even just the threat of doing so, further strengthened its position with both the private label and brand name producers.

The growth of the A&P chain and its imitators in the teens and on into the Roaring Twenties inflicted the first telling wound in the viability of the small independent grocery store. The manufacturers of national brands maintained strong advertising programs to compete now with both private label and chain store brands. Overall, this helped the independents, their major outlet. At the same time, this ceaseless promotion pressured the chains to also carry these higher priced goods. In time the chains expanded their name brand offerings, but they could buy at the best wholesale prices and pass the savings (often over the producers' objections) on to their customers. This further diminished the ability of the independents to compete. It was an independent grocer, nevertheless, who conceived the method for exploiting the power of the brand name which ultimately revolutionized America's grocery trade.

Charles Saunders of Memphis, Tennessee formulated a plan for turning heavy national brand advertising to his advantage. He recognized that this steady promotion was creating consumer demand which was not being adequately exploited. The name brands competed with the more profitable, to the proprietor, private label brands in independent stores. They also had to contend with the chains' lower priced store brands. This competitive situation is what had prompted the advertising in the first place. In 1916, Saunders opened a neighborhood store stocked exclusively with the best known, most vividly packaged and most heavily advertised national brands. To make sure he could offer the lowest possible prices he designed a no-frills store with a no credit, no deliveries policy similar to A&P's. He went one essential step further though by laying out his operation as a self-service store. The convention of retrieving all items for the customer was abandoned. Shoppers were given a wire basket and invited to fend for themselves.

Saunders' innovation went even beyond self-service, which had already been tried elsewhere in one form or another without much success. His market was, in effect, a one-way street. There was just one way into the store, and a single way out past the cashier. In between lay a single sinuous route which exposed the shopper to all of the store's departmentalized goods, all within easy reach. The store was totally devoted to offering name brands at low prices and letting them sell themselves. It worked. It worked so well, in fact, that Saunders applied for a patent on the one-way self-service format in 1917.

There was, and continues to be considerable speculation over the name Saunders chose for his new store. Whatever the allusions, literary or otherwise, it was undoubtedly intended for maximum impact and name recognition. The man who had recast the process of food shopping bestowed upon his invention the unlikely name of Piggly Wiggly.

The Piggly Wiggly concept was not universally embraced by American shoppers used to being served at least their groceries, if not credit or delivery. The Piggly Wigglys did soon spread, nevertheless, because there were enough people more concerned with savings than service, and because Saunders took a clever approach to sharing his format with other independent grocers. Instead of financing and building a chain of new stores as his fortunes allowed, he leased the whole system, including the Piggly Wiggly name, to independent entrepreneurs for 20% of gross. This made him very rich, very quickly. By 1920, when the Saunders patent was actually granted, Piggly Wiggly franchises were well established in Houston, Dallas, Cincinnati, Chicago and Richmond. At its peak, there were 2660 Piggly Wigglys, all selling products that sold themselves.

If Piggly Wiggly and its inevitable imitators accustomed Americans to low service/high value food shopping, the Depression paved the way for the expansion of this system to grand proportions. In 1930, Michael Cullen opened the first King Kullen in Queens, New York, ushering in the age of the supermarket. Cullen applied the self-service format to a store of expansive proportions, four to five times the size of a typical chain store. High volume/low margin selling coupled with an unprecedented variety of goods met the needs of the time. Cullen knew that low prices and a wide selection would entice thrifty customers. He also embellished the convolutions of the Piggly Wiggly aisle pattern to ensure that the shoppers would be exposed to all of the vast quantities of carefully departmentalized, strictly name brand goods. Satisfied with the bargain price of staples, the shopper was thereby presented with many other affordable, but higher margin items to purchase on impulse. This strategy worked exceedingly well (and still does).

Cullen could not depend on the great number of items in a store as big as his to necessarily sell themselves. The expanded choice which enabled value-based shopping no longer allowed strict dependence on the major manufacturers' advertising. The supermarket needed to build on this with its own promotions to compete with the chain stores and maintain the large customer base it required to be profitable. This gave birth to the concept of loss leaders. These were selected items advertised at or below cost to get the customers in the door. The money lost on loss leaders, and the minimal profit on staples, were more than balanced by the high margin impulse buys. National brand advertising moved from the leading edge of the grocery business to its foundation.

Cullen's "super" market was not an entirely new idea. One form or another of the large departmentalized, high volume self-service market had already existed for a number of years west of the Mississippi, particularly in southern California. King Kullen just opened in the proverbial right place at the right time. Its success, and that of the quick succession of other new supermarkets, made only slow converts of the grocery chains however. The year that Michael Cullen went into business was also the year A&P reached its peak of 15,737 stores, about 2600 more than the next four largest grocery chains combined.

Chain stores and supermarkets were both operated on the basis of high volume and low prices. Their fundamental differences, however, lent advantage to the supermarket in Depression-afflicted America. The chains were relatively small, conveniently located neighborhood stores. They had been designed for visits by foot and frequent small purchases in the days before refrigerators and automobiles became commonplace. In the 1930's, Americans appreciated the even lower prices and much greater selection of the supermarkets. These stores were designed for a mobile society which preferred less frequent, but much larger grocery purchases. Because of their size, the supermarkets were located away from the neighborhoods, and on less expensive commercial land where there was room for a large building and expansive parking lot. Their size, selection and accessibility by car also meant that fewer of the supermarkets were needed to service a given geographical area. Cullen himself estimated that one King Kullen served the customer base of ten A&Ps. Inevitably, this captured the attention of the Great Atlantic & Pacific Tea Company.

The supermarkets challenged the chain stores with as radical a shift in retailing as the chains had presented to the independent grocers a generation earlier. By the very nature of their size and the investment they had in their own way of doing business, the chains naturally resisted this new way of selling. Supermarkets spread only slowly at first, and so remained a worry rather than a threat for a few years. By mid-decade, however, their growth appeared to be geometric. There were about 300 supermarkets in 1935, 1200 by the end of the following year.

To its credit, A&P, the largest of the chains by far, was the first to respond to the dictates of change. In 1936 it opened 20 supermarkets and closed 200 of its conventional stores. In 1937, it added 262 supermarkets at the cost of 1700 neighborhood stores. The A&P supermarkets of necessity gave name brands equal footing with their own. A&P's merchandising expertise, nevertheless, guaranteed profit from both. In 1938, A&P made the strategic commitment to transform itself once more, this time into a chain of supermarkets. Within a decade, most other grocery chains either followed or perished. Brand names and advertising had proven unbeatable.

COMMERCE, SODA STYLE

The success and growth of bicarbonate of soda among the shifting sands of distribution and promotion of goods was founded on the foresight, or just common sense, of John Dwight. In 1846, when packaged and branded goods were more an oddity than the norm, Dwight's Saleratus was offered as a product of such quality and value that the producer was willing to put his name on it and stand behind it. By clearly knowing his target market and his product, he was on his way to both defining and securing the consumer market for sodium bicarbonate.

Whether or not his decision was inspired by the success of Babbitt's bagged product, Dwight correctly identified the growing need of saleratus for leavening, and determined to meet that need with a superior quality, lower priced product than was otherwise available. He also appreciated the value of brand loyalty. Dwight accommodated many early customers by filling orders with their name on the label, but soon realized this would undermine any chances for growth. The 1, 1/2 and 1/4 pound packages for retail trade were thereafter offered exclusively as Dwight's Saleratus. The early success of Dwight's Saleratus was, in turn, an obvious lesson to the Church brothers, prompting, no doubt, the ready adoption of the Arm & Hammer logo for their Bicarbonate of Soda.

John Dwight and the Church brothers were determined to stand squarely behind their respective products. Their sodas were distributed only in part by wholesalers to the grocery and apothecary trades. Through fiscal conservatism and measured growth, both companies maintained their own sales force, despite limited resources. Promotion likewise took a different track, as it became apparent that the most effective way to develop sales to the increasingly literate consumer was through education.

Dwight's Saleratus, Arm & Hammer Bicarbonate of Soda, and later Dwight's Soda, Cow Brand (the term "baking" was not actually affixed to soda until sometime after the turn of the century) were all geared directly to the consumer via the general store or grocery. Where practical, these were served personally by Dwight & Co. and Church & Co. salesmen. Both companies relied on free recipe booklets and leaflets to communicate with their customers and the personal attention of their salesmen in courting the store owners.

In the 1880's, with the success of its approach proven in the U.S., John Dwight & Co. decided to investigate the market for cartons of Cow Brand in Canada. Except for a small local sale of packaged saleratus near Toronto, the Dominion had to that point relied chiefly on bulk sodium bicarbonate from England. Cow Brand caught on quickly in the English speaking provinces, and eventually in Quebec as well.

Outside the urban centers, the soda salesman himself was the most prominent and enduring form of advertising for the latter part of the 19th century. In the style more commonly associated with the patent medicine shows of that era, the soda salesman's horse and cart would be decorated with sign-bearing blankets, bunting, flags, plumes, and anything else that might catch the eye and attract attention. Promotional posters would be nailed in all strategic locations, and free leaflets made available at the general store or grocery. These would share the best baking ideas, plus non-food household uses that had been suggested by some of the more inventive bicarbonate users. The consumer interest in inventing new uses for sodium bicarbonate was in obvious harmony with the American spirit. This more than anything seems to have accelerated the poularity of the product well beyond what would have been expected based on its intended use. Consumer invention, the folk uses, would sustain the growth in retail sales throughout the 20th century.

The soda salesman's job was to raise interest and excitement among the townspeople, thereby creating demand. He then had to convince the local store owner to stock Arm & Hammer or Cow Brand to profit from that demand. Although lacking in the flair of proponents of the well known "snake oils" of the day, like Kickapoo Indian Sagwa, the soda salesmen did effectively lay the foundation for an enduring demand for their product. This endurance was founded, of course, on quality and performance rather than a pitchman's hype. The Kickapoo's medicine shows are now long forgotten, along with Hostetter's Celebrated Stomach Bitters, the venerable Lydia Pinkham's Vegetable Compound and other famous remedies of the day. Baking soda has meanwhile prospered, arguably rivaled in endurance only by Dr. Mile's Compound Extract of Tomato (now known as catsup).

By the 1890's, the use of sodium bicarbonate in baking was so widespread, either as a separate ingredient or as a component of baking powder, that a number of manufacturers had entered the bicarb business. This naturally put pressure on the sales of the packaged products from the two major producers. Some storekeepers were even still willing to push bicarb from a barrel if they thought there was more profit in it. By sticking to their own proven approach to distribution and promotion, both the Dwight and Church companies established and expanded their respective consumer constituencies. Dedicated salesmen, free recipe books, leaflets sharing the new uses of soda, and later the trading cards that became the rage among consumers, all complemented a sales effort based on an inherently high quality, high value product. This approach, stimulating demand and encouraging inventive uses, was uniquely effective. At the close of the 19th century, Arm & Hammer and Cow Brand were the country's two leading brands of bicarbonate of soda, fixtures in the conventional grocery store and ready to profit from the coming changes in the grocery business.

The era of self-service markets started by Piggly Wiggly was tailor made for the consumer franchise which had been so firmly established by the two dominant name brand baking sodas. They were as necessary as clothespins and as distinctively packaged as Campbell's Soup. Food merchandising A&P style proved no threat to these brand leaders, most likely because they were so well established and low priced to begin with that the steady but relatively low volume of business they represented was not worth pursuing with a store brand. From the start, A&P itself pursued the baking powder market instead. This was, in fact, its first manufactured item, in 1891. This was an entirely reasonable choice since baking powder use was growing without an entrenched brand, while bicarb was already an inexpensive household staple. With the supermarket age and the ultimate ascendancy of the name brand, baking soda's shelf space was impregnable.

COMPETITION

Success breeds competition, and the success of the Dwight and Church companies in the consumer market attracted the attention of manufacturers both large and small. In the 1870's, James Pyle started repacking bulk imported bicarb in New York as Dietetic Saleratus, but lost interest in cultivating this business after introducing a washing and cleansing powder named Pearline. He, like B.T. Babbitt before him, apparently saw a greater future in cleaning than in baking. Also during the 1870's, Herrick Allen began selling Gold Medal Saleratus from Syracuse, eventually incorporating his brother-in-law, J. Monroe Taylor, and a small South Brooklyn factory into his business. Trade was initially good, but Gold Medal was discontinued in the 1890's after several years of waning sales. From 1870 to the mid-1890's, Deland and Co. produced saleratus in Fairport, New York, giving up only after the Church and Dwight companies pre-empted competition with exclusive claim to a new manufacturing technology. During the 1880's, an ex-employee of Church & Co., William Patton, convinced Alexander Howell, a producer of condensed milk, to manufacture bicarbonate of soda. This venture lasted only a few years.

The most formidable competition to both Church & Co. and John Dwight & Co. was the large and prosperous Pennsylvania Salt Manufacturing Co., producer of lye, soda ash, a range of other alkalies, acids, organic chemicals and oil. In 1865, the year in which Austin Church retired from John Dwight & Co., PennSalt contracted with the Kryolith Co. of Copenhagen to import 6000 tons per year of their Greenland cryolite, a sodium aluminum flouride mineral. This was to be processed into alkali products according to Kryolith technology. By 1867, the founding year of Church & Co., PennSalt's cryolite-derived products included high quality sodium bicarbonate.

Although PennSalt's resources dwarfed those of the Dwight and Church companies combined, and despite the fine quality of their sodium bicarbonate, they competed less effectively in the consumer market than in bulk industrial sales. As a diversified manufacturer of heavy chemicals for industry, their bicarb and consumer saleratus business could hardly command the commitment that the two dedicated producers could provide.

PennSalt had inadvertently done John Dwight a favor, of sorts, in 1870 by appropriating Elihu Church's package art for Dwight's Saleratus, since this resulted in Dwight's very successful Cow Brand. PennSalt was to impact as well the fortunes of Arm & Hammer Bicarbonate of Soda as a result of the 1891 fire at the Church & Co. plant. The cryolite-derived bicarb was of such high quality that Church & Co. purchased it to supplement the supply from John Dwight & Co. until the factory was rebuilt.

It took until the 1880's for a competitor with the potential to seriously jeopardize Arm & Hammer and Cow Brand sodas to finally appear. This company succeeded, instead, in reuniting the descendants of John Dwight and Austin Church and solidifying the position of their products in the home.

REUNITED

In 1863, while Dr. Church was still producing saleratus for his brother-in-law, Ernest Solvay had made commercially viable in Belgium a new process for the production of soda ash. Using salt, limestone and ammonia, his process produced a relatively pure sodium bicarbonate which was then converted by heating to sodium carbonate. The Solvay process took more than two decades to reach the U.S., until 1884 when the Solvay Process Co. built a soda ash plant near Syracuse, New York. In 1887, after Church-process bicarb was already well established nationwide, the Solvay plant began producing sodium bicarbonate for local industrial customers. This Solvay product was not at first suitable for consumer use, however, because of a slight ammonia odor.

Eventually the operators of the Solvay plant learned how to produce a fine quality sodium bicarbonate by dissolving their soda ash and reacting it with carbon dioxide gas. The resulting food grade, low cost bicarb enjoyed only very modest consumer sales, however. This was due mostly to lack of support from Solvay itself. Retail bicarbonate was a very minor business for a soda ash plant geared to large industrial markets. Solvay was not committed to effectively compete with the well established and well supported Arm & Hammer and Cow Brand sodas.

As the first domestic source of soda ash, the Solvay plant naturally attracted the attention of both the Dwight and Church companies, since this would be a new and less expensive source of sodium carbonate for their process. When it became apparent that Solvay bicarbonate could in time be made with superior quality and sold for less per pound than the dry carbonation production costs, Church & Co. decided to try the new technology itself. In 1889, an experimental plant was set up in Greenpoint, but it proved to be a failure.

Two years later, in February of 1891, the fire at the Arm & Hammer plant forced Church & Co. to rely on John Dwight & Co. for most of its needs, and PennSalt for the rest, in order to stay in business until resumption of production in November. In June of that year, Church & Co. and John Dwight & Co. jointly entered into a five year supply contract for the full output of Solvay's bicarb plant, minus a minor amount previously committed. This provided both companies the added security of an additional source of high quality sodium bicarbonate. It also turned a potentially threatening competitor, especially in bulk sales, into a supplier.

Solvay process bicarb was used to supplement rather than replace their own production since it could not be produced in sufficient quantity to satisfy the entire demand. The two companies kept their plants in full operation while gaining experience with the new supply. In 1894, Church & Co. decided to build its own Solvay process plant dedicated solely to the production of sodium bicarbonate. This might have been motivated by concern over the scheduled expiration of the

Solvay Process Co. supply contract in June of 1896. If the contract was not renewed, Solvay would have a market-proven and accepted product which it could sell itself, or through contract with a competitor to the Church and Dwight companies.

The Church brothers were also undoubtedly aware of the fact that John B. Ford, one of the principals in the Pittsburgh Plate Glass Co., had built a Solvay process soda ash plant in Wyandotte, Michigan in 1891. He was interested in soda ash for the U.S. glass industry, since it was becoming obvious that demand would soon exceed the Solvay Process Co.'s ability to supply. It was reasonable to believe that if the Syracuse plant could produce top quality bicarb, Ford's plant would eventually be able to as well. This concern proved to be well founded, although it was not until 1897 that the first sodium bicarbonate plant was built in Wyandotte.

In 1895, under the direction of James Church, the contributor of the Arm & Hammer logo, Church & Co. erected a small Solvay process plant in Trenton, Michigan, where the requisite raw materials occurred in adequate supply. The plant was dedicated to the production of sodium bicarbonate, rather than soda ash, but production was plagued by the residual ammonia smell. The Solvay company's additional steps of forming the soda ash and then producing the final purified bicarbonate were not known to Church. Before an entirely satisfactory and economical product could be produced, James Church died, and with him the determination to make the new plant a success.

The year 1896 served to Church & Co. a personal loss, and a manufacturing failure. Family ties, nevertheless, were to prove much stronger than business rivalries. The descendants of Austin Church and John Dwight, having seen the founders' vision of a consumer market for high quality saleratus so successfully realized, decided in that year that their two families should simply be reunited in business. To the merger Church & Co. brought Arm & Hammer Bicarbonate of Soda, the country's leading brand, while John Dwight & Co. brought Cow Brand and the Canadian market. The supply contract with the Solvay Process Co. was renewed, as it would be periodically well into the 20th century. Fifty years after John Dwight first sold Austin Church's saleratus to New York City merchants, the Church & Dwight Company was formed.

The packaging and shipping facilities that Dwight & Co. had been constructing next to the Solvay plant in Syracuse were expanded to meet the consolidated needs of Arm & Hammer and Cow Brand sodas. Although the two companies were now joined and the sodium bicarbonate was from one source, the two brands were kept distinct to capitalize on the consumer loyalty each had earned over the years. The growth of baking soda under both names in the 20th century proved the soundness of this decision.

The power of brand loyalty was amply demonstrated many years later. When Cow Brand Baking Soda was discontinued in the U. S., some time after the second world war, it dominated the metropolitan New York area, its birthplace. This was despite the fact that Arm & Hammer was by far the leading brand in the rest of the country, and care had been taken by the manufacturer to make clear that the baking soda contained in the two different packages was identical. Generations of New York homemakers had come to depend on their Cow Brand, and they stuck with it till the end. Cow Brand likewise remained the dominant baking soda in Canada until 1992, when this trademark was finally replaced with Arm & Hammer.

BAKING AND BEYOND

The second half of the 19th century had seen the timely

introduction of domestic sodium bicarbonate, followed by an acceptance and growth prompted by the complex merging of societal, cultural, technological, and even religious influences, some subtle, but in aggregate most effective. The religious underpinnings of the health food movement led to a concern over the purity and integrity of the foods eaten by those seeking to settle and make prosper a rapidly developing new nation. This worked against baking powders and yeast - temporarily and certainly not mortally, but just enough for baking soda to ensure its place in the market.

The railroads became the backbone of the country, transforming it into a world class grain producer and fostering the rise of American style mass merchandising. Packaging, trademarks, advertising and distribution developed in such an amazingly complementary fashion that those companies like Dwight's and Church's that were savy enough to take advantage established themselves securely for the changes which awaited them in 20th century America.

Baking soda rode the wave of progress in the 19th century to become established as indispensible in the home. The versatility of low cost/high quality baking soda led consumers to discover a wide variety of uses beyond leavening nearly from its start and on into the early 20th century, while its use in home baking was still strong. As baking in the home eventually declined, these folk uses would grow and fill the void, ultimately to be supplemented by a variety of unique industrial applications. Austin Church would undoubtedly be amazed, and John Dwight, pleased.

TWO

The

Household

Alternative

How do you keep people from running away from your running shoes? (see page 81)

TWO

THE HOUSEHOLD ALTERNATIVE

The blend of American ingenuity and Yankee frugality during the first century or so of its commercial existence produced an incredible range of uses for baking soda around the home. Baking soda was, above all, a pure and inexpensive staple and an old standby for baking. Until fairly recently, "make do" was the ethic spurring application of baking soda to tasks undreamed by Austin Church and John Dwight. There may have been a name brand scouring powder, tooth powder, kitchen cleaner, or mouthwash at the local grocery store, but the clever and thrifty homemaker could make do with the ever reliable baking soda. More often than not, making do provided fine results. And, in true American fashion, making do was seen as a test of resourcefulness rather than a reflection of low economic status. Homemakers started writing to the bicarb producers, and later to newspaper and magazine columnists with their latest brainstorm for how to use baking soda for nearly everything but baking.

In the past two decades, environmental concerns have caused a shift in focus for baking soda use. The smart and economical alternative to scores of specialized powders and potions for home and personal care has become the safe and natural alternative as well. Baking soda's versatility, purity, safety and simplicity have recommended it to those who prefer to avoid organic solvents, harsh chemicals and suspect chemical additives in the products used in their homes.

The reason that home use continues to grow is that regardless of the user's motivation, baking soda in most cases is an effective alternative to the sophisticated formulated products it so easily replaces. It's used because it works. Despite the fact that virtually all of the folk uses of baking soda were, by definition, developed and promulgated by users in the home, there are sound scientific reasons why it is so effective in so many different applications.

BAKING SODA BUFFERS

The basis of most of baking soda's uses is its fundamental chemical nature. As sodium bicarbonate, $NaHCO_3$, baking soda can be alternately described as sodium acid carbonate. It is a compound of the strongly basic sodium cation (Na^+) and the not quite as strongly acidic carbonic acid anion (HCO_3^-). The result is a weakly basic (slightly alkaline) compound with a pH in solution of approximately 8. The pH symbol is used to express a solution's acidity, neutrality or alkalinity on a continuous scale of 0 to 14, with pH 7 being neutral. Solutions from pH 7 to pH 0 are increasingly acidic. Solutions from pH 7 to pH 14 are increasingly alkaline. In water, baking soda gives slightly alkaline, nearly neutral solutions. It is an effective buffer as well. It tries to maintain solutions at its own pH, so that more acidic substances are raised in pH, and more alkaline substances are decreased in pH. In this way, baking soda can act as either an acid or base itself. In the presence of acids it acts as a neutralizing base. In the presence of bases it acts as a neutralizing acid. This dual nature accounts for many of baking soda's uses.

Unquestionably, the most important use to which we all put the buffering properties of baking soda is the one we are born with

- the bicarbonate ion is the naturally occurring component of blood which maintains its delicate acid/alkaline balance. One of the oldest man-made uses is as a treatment for indigestion. Baking soda effectively neutralizes stomach acids and helps to relieve heartburn. The buffering effect of baking soda is also the key to a number of household applications. Added to swimming pool water, baking soda maintains the correct pH and alkalinity for optimum chlorine effectiveness. Likewise, it can provide the required pH-controlled environment for refuse-destroying bacteria in the home septic system.

BAKING SODA CLEANS

Baking soda is a triple threat cleaner, supplying detergency, gentle abrasion and effervescence. Its mildly alkaline nature is the basis of its gentle cleansing action. Most dirt and grease contain fatty acids which will react with baking soda to form a soap. This soap in turn works to remove the rest of the dirt or grease components. While stronger alkalis, like lye or lye-based products, can produce more cleaning power, they are not nearly as safe as baking soda on soiled surfaces or the user's hands. These alkalis are generally toxic or irritating as well.

Baking soda provides gentle abrasion in paste form, or dry on a damp sponge or toothbrush. The dissolved portion provides detergency for the soil lifted by the soft undissolved crystals. These crystals are softer than nearly any surface and break down readily in use, actually providing more polishing than abrasion. Baking soda cannot scratch most household surfaces, and is often used with soaps and detergents to enhance their cleaning power. Besides reacting with soils to form cleansing soaps and physically lifting soil particles by gentle abrasion, baking soda can produce effervescent bubbles to lift dirt from most surfaces. All that's needed is baking soda, water and a common kitchen acid like vinegar.

Baking soda's unique combination of cleaning effects has made it the safe cleaning alternative around the home for nearly everything from stained kitchen sinks, to mildewed shower tile, to teeth.

BAKING SODA DEODORIZES

Most deodorizers work either as a perfume (like a room deodorizer) to mask odors, or an absorbent (like charcoal or coffee grounds) to physically entrap odors. Perfumes do not eliminate unpleasant odors; they just overpower them with a more acceptable scent. Absorbents eventually come to equilibrium with the air and release some of the odor originally contained. Baking soda neutralizes odors in the air in much the same way that it neutralizes chemicals in solution. Many objectionable odors are either strongly acidic, like sour milk, or strongly basic, like spoiled fish. Baking soda deodorizes by chemically reacting with acidic or basic odor molecules and irreversibly converting them to a neutral, more odor-free state.

Baking soda works best in a confined and somewhat humid space, such as a refrigerator, car trunk or closet. Its deodorizing efficiency depends on how much odor it has to deal with and how long it has to work. The longer air is in contact with baking soda, the more odor neutralization takes place. In the refrigerator, an open box of baking soda will be effective for about three months.

Baking soda deodorizes in solution much as it does in the air. Solutions used as a mouthwash, a cutting board cleaner or a hand cleaner will neutralize, for example, acidic onion and garlic odors and basic fish odors.

BAKING SODA EXTINGUISHES FIRES

In the presence of high heat, baking soda decomposes to sodium carbonate (soda ash), water and carbon dioxide. It was long theorized that baking soda is effective against electrical and grease fires because of this released carbon dioxide, which is heavier than air and smothers the fire by displacing the oxygen on which it feeds, and because of the water released, which cools the fire below the ignition temperature. Although baking soda is the only household chemical effective against these fires, recent research has shown that this is more likely due to complicated chemical reactions occurring in the flames themselves. Baking soda can be used on electrical (Class C) fires in equipment and wiring, and flammable liquids (Class B) fires involving grease, gasoline, oils and solvents. It is not recommended for fires involving ordinary combustibles (Class A), like paper, cloth, wood and plastics because they can reignite. Water is the most effective extinguisher for these. Conversely, water should not be used on Class B fires, which it can actually spread, or on Class C fires, due to danger of electrical shock. Commercial dry chemical, foam and soda/water fire extinguishers all contain baking soda. Many homeowners keep handy a box of baking soda in case of kitchen, garage or automobile fires.

BAKING SODA WORKS

Over the years, scores of baking soda uses have been disseminated by newspapers, magazines and word-of-mouth. No one, until now, has ever collected and published these for handy reference. So whether your motivation is ecology, frugality or ingenuity, the following more or less complete list of the folk uses of baking soda is for you.

Many jobs in the home are handled by baking soda alone in one of three forms:

Dry - Sprinkle baking soda straight from the box.

Paste - Mix three parts baking soda with one part water.

Solution - Dissolve four tablespoons baking soda in one quart of water.

In the uses that follow, one or more of these forms is recommended for scores of jobs. Many uses recommend baking soda together with other ingredients readily available in the home or from the grocery or hardware store.

Although all of the formulas which follow are believed to be safe for their intended use, common sense and normal care are required. If there is any question about the colorfastness or delicacy of a soiled surface, try the formula on a small, inconspicuous part first. Every ingredient, even everyday kitchen items like salt and vinegar, should be handled with respect to avoid irritation to eyes and skin. When cleaning with any composition, whether as innocuous as baking soda or aggressive as a heavy duty commercial toilet bowl cleaner, it is good practice to wear skin and eye protection. All chemicals should be kept out of the reach of children.

Any formulas suggested for personal care use should be tested first on a small patch of skin, the inside of the forearm for instance, if there is any concern of sensitization or allergic reaction. It is also recommended that all containers and mixing equipment for personal care formulas, especially those used near the eyes, should be sterilized or at least meticulously washed. If there are any reservations about the use of a composition in the eyes or on broken skin, seek the advice of a health care professional. The prudent approach to compositions used by or on people pertains as well to those intended for animals.

The formulas and suggestions presented here are for the most part those that baking soda users have developed in their own homes over the years and found safe and effective enough to pass on. Many sources have been investigated to make this collection as comprehensive as possible, with editing only as necessary to maintain a reasonably consistent format. Our purpose has been to compile as many of the purportedly safe and effective consumer-developed uses of baking soda as possible, not to test and evaluate the merits of each. In the course of the 130 or so years over which these uses have been proposed, the motivation of their "inventors" have ranged from using baking soda as the best choice among very few for the task, to using baking soda as the most acceptable alternative to more effective, but less environmentally conscionable preparations. While baking soda is indeed a viable alternative to some of today's highly formulated chemical concoctions, be aware that it might require a little more elbow grease for satisfactory results, or might not in fact work as well. Quite a bit of chemistry, after all, went into making those concoctions as convenient and powerful as possible. Then again, that's why some people prefer to use baking soda instead.

Anyone who has discovered a use for baking soda that is not presented here is cordially invited to pass it along via the publisher. You'll have our appreciation, and the satisfaction of continuing a tradition started in your great-grandmother's time.

BAKING SODA IN THE KITCHEN

Rubber Glove Lubricant
It's good practice to wear rubber gloves for chores using any type of chemical cleaners or polishes. If you have trouble sliding your hands into the gloves, sprinkle in a little baking soda to ease the way.

Drain Cleaners
Kitchen drains collect grease and assorted organic matter. When

clogged, they must be opened by breaking up and dissolving the gunk with highly caustic lye or lye based products. Drains can be prevented from clogging by periodic cleaning with baking soda alone or in combination with salt and common cooking acids.

DRAIN CLEANER I

1 lb. baking soda
1 lb. salt

Blend well and store in an airtight container. Periodically pour 1 cup down the drain followed by 1 quart of boiling water. Allow to sit for several hours or overnight, then flush with hot tap water.

DRAIN CLEANER II

2 cups baking soda
2 cups salt
½ cup cream of tartar

Blend well and store in an airtight container. Periodically pour ¼ cup down the drain followed by 1 cup of boiling water. Allow to sit for about five minutes and then flush with hot tap water.

DRAIN CLEANER III

½ cup baking soda
½ cup vinegar

Pour the baking soda down the drain followed by the vinegar. Let sit for about two hours; be careful in case the bubbling action causes splashing. Flush with hot tap water.

Scouring Powders
Baking soda on a damp sponge will tackle many jobs in place of commercial abrasive scouring powders and is among the

safest cleaners for stains in colored porcelain sinks. For tougher jobs, you can blend the following ahead of time and have them ready when needed.

GENTLE SCOURING POWDER
1 cup baking soda
1 cup borax
1 cup salt

Blend well and store in a covered container.

TOUGH SCOURING POWDER
1 cup baking soda
1 cup borax
1 cup finely powdered pumice or chalk

Blend well and store in a covered container. The natural pumice abrasive makes this suitable for heavy duty jobs. Pumice is quite abrasive, however, so take care to avoid scratching.

Food Container Deodorant
Glass and plastic storage containers for food and beverages sometimes absorb odors from their contents. These odors can often be eliminated by first washing the container well and then adding 2 tablespoons of baking soda and filling with hot water. After shaking well to dissolve the baking soda, the container should be covered and allowed to soak for a couple of hours, overnight for especially strong odors. The container should then be washed. This deodorizing treatment can be used for milk and juice pitchers, Thermos® bottles, picnic jugs, ice chests, lunch boxes, ice buckets, ice cube trays, crisper boxes, all plastic containers, and virtually any other glass or plastic device designed to contain food or drink.

When storing seasonal items, like picnic jugs and ice chests, add some baking soda before closing to keep them smelling fresh.

Coffee Pot Cleaner
Glass and stainless steel coffee pots can be washed with a solution of four tablespoons of baking soda in one quart of water. For badly stained pots, scrub with a paste of three parts baking soda per one part water or soak with a solution of four tablespoons baking soda per quart of hot water. **Aluminum coffee or cooking pots should not be washed with any hot alkaline substance, including hot baking soda solution, because it will discolor or pit this metal.**

Coffee Maker Cleaner
Fill the reservoir with a solution of four tablespoons baking soda per quart of water and run the coffee maker through one cycle. Remove the aluminum filter basket first, if so equipped. Follow with two additional cycles using plain water each time. Exterior plastic surfaces can be cleaned as well with a baking soda solution or scrub.

Burnt-On Food Softener
Food stuck or burned onto pots, pans and casseroles of all compositions **except aluminum** can be softened for easy removal by first covering liberally with baking soda. Add enough hot or boiling water to cover and let soak for about ten minutes, longer for stubborn soils. For especially tough messes, boil a solution of one tablespoon baking soda per cup of water in the cookware. After the burnt residue is softened it can be readily removed with additional dampened baking soda and a nylon scrubber.

Non-Stick Cookware Cleaner
Non-stick cookware is popular, among other reasons, for being notoriously easy to keep clean. Nevertheless, if not cleaned thoroughly, buildup of grease and oil will leave stains that will reduce the coating's effectiveness. The following treatment is simple and effective.

TEFLON®/SIlVERSTONE® CLEANER

2 tablespoons baking soda
½ cup white vinegar
1 cup water

Add the ingredients to the utensil, place on stove and boil for ten minutes. Use the stove hood fan to minimize exposure to vinegar fumes. Wash as usual and re-season with salad oil.

Coffee/ Tea Stain Remover

Coffee and tea stains can be removed from plasic cups and dishes, china, cutting boards, butcher block and plastic laminate countertops by sprinkling on baking soda and scouring with a damp sponge. This will also work for light burns on china and butcherblock. For especially tough stains on plastic laminate, cover with lemon juice, let soak for 45 minutes, then sprinkle on baking soda and rub with a damp sponge. Rinse well.

Oven Cleaner

Lye based oven cleaners are perhaps the most dangerous household cleaning products. A standard oven (**not** self-cleaning or continuous clean) can be cleaned when cold with a paste of three parts baking soda per one part water, a nylon scrubber, and plenty of elbow grease. For particularly tough stains, use equal parts baking soda and salt in the paste. In electric ovens, be careful not to get any type of chemical, whether commercial cleaner, baking soda or salt, on the heating elements because they can easily corrode when heated and short out.

Stove Top Parts And Surface Cleaners

To clean burnt-on spills, enamel and stainless steel burner catch pans can be boiled in a nonaluminum pan for a few minutes in a solution of one tablespoon baking soda per quart of water. This works for the cast iron burners on gas stoves too. Grease and burnt-on food can be cleaned from stove tops with a baking soda scrub.

Microwave Oven Cleaner
If your microwave is overdue for a good cleaning, mix two tablespoons of baking soda into one cup of water in a one quart microwave safe bowl. Let this solution boil in the microwave for a few minutes so that the steam condenses on the inside walls. Wipe off the walls, inside of the door and the door seal with paper toweling followed by a damp cloth or sponge.

White Appliance and Sink Bleach
When white enameled metal appliances or white porcelain sinks start to yellow try the following. This contains bleach so be careful that it does not come into contact with paper, cloth, vinyl, pets, children etc., and that you use gloves and proper ventilation. **Do not use this on colored appliances or colored sinks.**

WHITE APPLIANCE & SINK BLEACH
¼ cup baking soda
½ cup bleach
1 quart warm water

Mix together well. Apply with a sponge, let set for about ten minutes, rinse well and dry.

Appliance Cleaners/ Deodorizers
Remove the top from a box of baking soda and label the box with a date three months away. Place the box on a refrigerator shelf and replace on the indicated date. Pour the used box in the garbage to deodorize or down the drain or garbage disposal to clean and remove odors.

Sprinkle some baking soda on the bottom of the automatic dishwasher to control odors between washing campaigns.

To remove stains, films and odors from the insides of refrigerators, freezers and automatic dishwashers use a scour of baking soda on a damp sponge, rinse well and dry.

To keep the door gaskets on refrigerators, freezers and automatic dishwashers clean and mildew-free, wash periodically with a solution of four tablespoons baking soda per quart of water.

Liquid Dishwashing Detergent Booster
Some liquid detergents for hand dishwashing don't have the grease cutting power they should. This can be easily improved by adding two tablespoons of baking soda to hot water in the dishpan along with the detergent. For particularly tough stuck on food, sprinkle baking soda on the area and scour with a nylon scrubber.

Kitchen Grease Remover
Try this cleaner for those dried-on grease spots on painted (enamel) cabinets, stove tops and stove backsplashes.

GREASE CUTTER

¼ cup baking soda
½ cup white vinegar
1 cup ammonia
1 gallon hot water

Mix well. Use rubber gloves and maintain adequate ventilation. For painted surfaces, try on a small area first to ensure that the cleaner will not discolor the paint; this is intended for glossy enamel painted surfaces and might attack normal flat interior paint. Wash the cabinets with the cleaner and a sponge, rinse with clear water and dry well. For stove tops and backsplashes the same procedure can be followed except that a nylon scrubber can be carefully used on particularly stubborn spots.

Baby High Chair Cleaner
Baby's high chair can be safely cleaned and deodorized after

every feeding with a solution of four tablespoons baking soda per quart of water. For dried-on accumulations around tray rails, chair spindles etc., try scrubbing with baking soda on a damp sponge or nylon scrubber.

Sponge/ Scrubber Cleaner
To renew and deodorize soiled kitchen sponges, nylon scrubbers, and scrub brushes, soak overnight in a solution of four tablespoons baking soda per quart of water.

Cutting Board Deodorizer
Wood and butcherblock breadboards and cutting boards that have picked up fish, onion or garlic odors can be deodorized by scrubbing with a paste of three parts baking soda per one part water followed by thorough rinsing and drying. For really strong odors, leave the paste on for about ten minutes before rinsing.

Hand Deodorizer
Onion, garlic and fish scent on hands can be neutralized by wetting the hands, sprinkling on baking soda, rubbing well, and then rinsing and drying.

Heel Mark Remover
Black heel marks on kitchen linoleum or vinyl flooring can be removed with baking soda on a damp sponge or nylon scrubber.

Garbage Disposal Cleaner
With warm tap water running, turn on the disposal and pour in 1 cup of baking soda. Keep the water running until one minute after all the baking soda is gone. A periodic cleaning like this will keep the grinding mechanism grease-free.

BAKING SODA IN THE BATHROOM

Hard Surface Cleaners
Virtually any hard surface in the bathroom can be cleaned with baking soda in place of solvent or caustic based commercial preparations. For routine cleaning of plastic laminate countertops and backsplashes, ceramic tile, porcelain or fiberglass sinks, tubs and showers, chrome fixtures, glass shower doors and mirrors, just scrub with baking soda on a damp sponge, rinse well and dry. Baking soda is one of the safest "abrasives" on fiberglass. For tough stains on bathroom surfaces, cover with lemon juice and let soak for about 30 minutes; then scrub with baking soda on a damp sponge, rinse well and dry. If the tile or fiberglass walls of your tub/shower enclosure are particularly filmy from soap scum, try the following:

DOUBLE DUTY SOAP SCUM CLEANER
¼ cup baking soda
½ cup vinegar
1 cup ammonia
1 gallon warm water

Mix well. Use rubber gloves and maintain adequate ventilation. Instead of getting in the tub or shower enclosure, use a sponge mop to apply this mixture liberally to the filmy walls. Rinse well.

Shower Curtain Cleaners
Spot cleaning of mildew on shower curtains requires only a baking soda scrub with a sponge, nylon scrubber or scrub brush.

Some plastic shower curtains are machine washable. Good results can be obtained by first filling the washer with warm water and then adding ½ cup laundry detergent or soap flakes, ½ cup baking soda, two bath towels (they provide scrubbing action) and the shower curtain. Run through the entire wash cycle and then add 1 cup of white vinegar to the rinse water. Do not rinse out the vinegar or spin dry. Remove the curtain from the machine and hang immediately to air dry. As the curtain dries the wrinkles will disappear.

Tile/ Grout Stain Removers
A simple baking soda paste is the first line of attack against rust stains on ceramic tile and mildew stains on grout. This is made from three parts baking soda per one part water. A nylon scrubber works well on tiles and an old toothbrush on grout. For especially tough stains, use household bleach in place of water to make the paste, being sure to wear rubber gloves and maintaining adequate ventilation. Rinse thoroughly.

Toilet Bowl Cleaners
Instead of using bleach, acid or lye based cleaners in your toilet bowl, try routine cleaning with baking soda and a toilet brush. For stained bowls, pour in ½ cup baking soda and ½ cup vinegar and scrub with a toilet brush. Be careful in case the effervescence causes splashing.

Bathroom Drain Cleaner
The following composition can be used to help dissolve scum and hair in sluggish bathroom sink and tub drains.

BATHROOM DRAIN FLUSH
1 cup baking soda
1 cup salt
½ cup white vinegar
2 quarts boiling water

Pour the baking soda, salt and vinegar into the drain. Let work for about 15 minutes; be careful in case the bubbling action causes splashing. Flush the drain with the boiling water, followed by hot tap water. The baking soda, salt and vinegar can also be used as a combination toilet bowl scrub and toilet drain cleaner.

Septic Tank Treatment

To keep your septic system working smoothly and to help avoid clogging, back-ups, corrosion and septic odors, flush one cup of baking soda down the toilet every week. It's necessary to add the baking soda on a regular basis since the dissolved sodium bicarbonate is forced out of the septic tank every time new material enters. Baking soda creates the optimum pH environment for bacterial digestion of household solid waste and clarification of the liquid leaving the septic tank for absorption in the soil of the drain field.

Grooming Aids Cleaner

Cosmetic sponges, combs, hair brushes, plastic curlers, and make-up applicators can be gently cleaned by soaking overnight in a solution of baking soda alone (four tablespoons baking soda per quart of water) or with a few drops of liquid soap. For natural bristle brushes, a tablespoon of clear ammonia can be added to the baking soda and liquid soap; use a covered container or adequate ventilation for soaking. Plastic combs can be cleaned and disinfected by using the simple baking soda solution with three tablespoons of household bleach added. Be careful this does not get on bleach sensitive surfaces; never mix bleach with liquid soap or ammonia.

BAKING SODA IN THE NURSERY

Baby Clothes Freshener

Baby clothes that have been stored a while (e.g. between arrivals) can be freshened without having to be laundered by briefly soaking in a solution of ½ cup baking soda per gallon of water, rinsing, and then gently drying.

Nursery Spotter
When baby leaves milk, food or spit-up stains on clothes, bibs, or bed clothes, pretreat with a paste of three parts baking soda per one part water until the item can be washed. This will also prevent the formation of sour odors.

Nursery Presoak
For items like dirty cloth diapers that require extra attention, presoak for an hour or two in a solution of ½ cup baking soda in 1 gallon of water.

Changing Pad Cleaner
Plastic changing pads can be routinely cleaned by wiping with a solution of one tablespoon baking soda per cup of water.

Diaper Pail Fresheners
Sprinkle each addition to the diaper pail liberally with baking soda to control odors until emptying.

When plastic diaper pails pick up odors, they can be cleaned and deodorized by adding 1 cup baking soda and then filling with warm water. Let this solution sit for an hour or two, then rinse and air dry.

Prickly Heat/ Diaper Rash Soother
Prickly heat can be soothed by giving the baby a sponge bath with a solution of one tablespoon baking soda per quart of water. After bathing, gently pat the baby dry with a soft towel.

This same solution can be used as a bath soak to soothe mild diaper rash.

Vomit Clean-up
If baby, or older child, vomits and you cannot clean it

immediately, cover it with baking soda to control the smell (and sight) until you can get to it.

Stuffed Toy Cleaner

Baby's favorite stuffed animals often seem to attract more than their share of dirt and smells. Unfortunately, most are not launderable. When it's time for a cleaning, place the stuffed toy in a large bag, add ½ cup of baking soda, close the bag and shake vigorously. Remove from the bag and shake as much baking soda as possible from the animal; remove the rest with a hairbrush.

Vinyl covered stuffed toys can be surface cleaned with a solution of one tablespoon baking soda per cup of water; stains can be removed with a little baking soda on a damp sponge.

Baby Bottle Deodorizer

To remove lingering sour milk or juice odors from baby bottles, add two tablespoons of baking soda, fill with hot water, shake or stir to dissolve the baking soda and let soak for at least a couple of hours, overnight if possible. Rinse well and wash as usual.

Crayon Remover

Crayon marks can be removed from washable walls and floors by gentle scrubbing with baking soda on a damp sponge or nylon scrubber.

BAKING SODA IN THE LAUNDRY

Fabric Softener

Whether you use synthetic detergents or soap flakes, adding ½ cup of baking soda to the wash load will make the clothes feel soft and smell fresh.

Fabric Freshener

For items that are smelly enough to require extra attention, such as cloth diapers, gardening clothes, or whatever you were wearing for that close encounter with the skunk, presoak for an hour or two in a solution of ½ cup baking soda in 1 gallon of water. This will help remove stains as well.

Ring-Around-The-Collar

As a prewash treatment for ring-around-the-collar, dirty cuffs and even mildew stains on stored clothing, scrub with a paste of three parts baking soda to two parts white vinegar. Maintain adequate ventilation.

Delicates

Hand washables and delicates that have acquired a stale odor in storage need not be laundered. Just soak in four tablespoons baking soda per quart of water, rinse well, squeeze and air dry.

Hand washables and delicates that do need laundering can be washed in a solution of one teaspoon mild liquid hand dishwashing detergent and two tablespoons baking soda per quart of water. Rinse and dry as usual.

Dry Cleanables

Many "dry clean only" items can be safely cleaned and freshened between visits to the cleaner's by washing in a solution of four tablespoons baking soda per quart of water, followed by thorough rinsing and gentle drying. Test for colorfastness first.

Hampers

Between laundering campaigns, hampers can be kept odor free by sprinkling baking soda on each layer of added clothing. This is especially effective with grimy work or athletic wear, and will keep the hamper itself from picking up odors. The baking soda added to the washing machine with the dirty clothes will also help them come out soft and smelling fresh.

Laundry Bluing
Before the days of fluorescent whiteners in laundry detergents, bluing was often used to make whites whiter. This was based on centuries of experience in the arts where it was discovered that adding a very small amount of blue will make white appear whiter. If you prefer to launder with soap flakes instead of synthetic detergents and would like some extra "natural" whitening, try the following:

LAUNDRY BLUING

$3\frac{1}{2}$ cups baking soda
1 cup corn syrup
$\frac{1}{2}$ teaspoon ultramarine blue

Mix well and store in a covered container. Use a scant $\frac{1}{2}$ teaspoon per load of whites. Mix into the water before adding the clothes. This is a dye so do not add directly to clothes.

BAKING SODA AROUND THE HOUSE

Room Deodorizer
A tobacco smoke filled room can be made more comfortable with a baking soda deodorizer spray. Fill a plant mister bottle with a solution of four tablespoons baking soda per quart of warm water. Mist the smoky air to reduce the haze and the smell.

Upholstery and Carpet Cleaners
Before using any cleaning preparation on carpeting or upholstery, first check colorfastness in an inconspicuous area.

Fresh oily or greasy stains on carpets and cloth upholstery can be absorbed with equal parts baking soda and salt or cleaned with a paste of three parts baking soda per one part water. Sprinkle the powder on the stain, brush lightly, leave for a few hours and then vacuum. Rub the paste into the stain, let dry, and then brush or vacuum away.

For coffee or tea stains try a solution of two tablespoons baking soda and one tablespoon borax per pint of water.

To clean and deodorize carpets and cloth upholstery, simply sprinkle on baking soda liberally, let sit for about fifteen minutes and then vacuum thoroughly. Be sure the carpet or upholstery is dry first. For particularly musty smells leave the baking soda on longer.

For carpets that are musty or mildewy from having been wet, dry thoroughly. Sprinkle baking soda liberally beneath (if not tacked) and on top. Let sit overnight before vacuuming. Repeat if necessary.

Vinyl Upholstery Cleaner
A solution of four tablespoons baking soda per quart of water, or baking soda sprinkled on a damp sponge will remove oils and grease that can embrittle vinyl. Follow with a clear water rinse and wipe dry.

Leather Mildew Remover
For mildewed leather (not suede) upholstery or clothing, rub on a paste of three parts baking soda to one part water, let dry overnight and gently brush or vacuum away. The leather will have to be repolished after this cleaning.

Multipurpose Cleaner
This is a cleaner for virtually any washable hard surface around the house, including windows, counters, appliances, tile floors and walls, marble table tops, vinyl floors, etc. It can also be used for spot cleaning spills and stains.

ALL-PURPOSE CLEANER

¼ cup baking soda
1 cup clear ammonia
½ cup white vinegar
1 gallon warm water

Mix well. Use rubber gloves and maintain adequate ventilation. Apply with a sponge, mop, or paper towel; rinse and dry. For stuck-on soils, use with a nylon scrubber. For windows and mirrors, wipe on cleaner with a paper towel, let dry to a powdery haze, and wipe clean with a dry paper towel.

Marble-Top Stains
Stained marble on furniture tops can be safely scoured with baking soda sprinkled on a damp sponge. After scrubbing, let the paste sit a few minutes before rinsing with warm water and drying.

Wax Remover
Crayon and other waxy marks, as from candles or paraffin, can be removed from most hard washable surfaces with a paste of three parts baking soda per one part water, and a nylon scrubber.

Ash Tray Treatment
Clean and deodorize ash trays with a solution of four tablespoons baking soda per quart of water. Then sprinkle some baking soda into the clean, dry ashtray to prevent smoldering and reduce the odor of ashes.

Litter Box Deodorant
Baking soda sprinkled on the bottom of the litter box before adding litter will help control odors. Use about 1 cup baking soda for each three pounds of litter.

If you can't attend to used litter as quickly as you would like, cover with baking soda and stir slightly. This should control odors for a couple of hours.

Pet Accident Deodorizer
If your pet has had an acccident or vomited in the house, there will be a lingering odor for the animal even if not for you. To avoid a repeat performance, clean the spot as quickly and thoroughly as possible. On carpeting and cloth upholstered furniture, sprinkle liberally when completely dry with baking soda, after checking for colorfastness. Let sit for 15 minutes and then vacuum thoroughly.

Dog Dry Cleaner
To clean and deodorize your dog when you can't give him a bath, rub baking soda thoroughly into his coat (make sure he's dry) and then brush it out.

Metal Cleaners
Baking soda can be used to clean and polish most metal fixtures and decorations in the home. Baking soda sprinkled on a damp sponge, or a simple paste of three parts baking soda per one part water will gently clean and polish chrome, stainless steel, silver and gold plating. **Do not use on decorative aluminum, or lacquered brass, bronze or copper.** For big or tough jobs, try the following.

ALL PURPOSE METAL CLEANER
1 cup baking soda
2½ cups washing soda (sodium carbonate)
½ cup trisodium phosphate (from the hardware store)

Mix well and store in a closed container. Trisodium phosphate is a skin irritant so be sure to wear rubber gloves while mixing and using. Sprinkle the powder on a damp sponge, gently scour the metal, rinse well and dry.

ASH METAL POLISH

Try this if you have a ready supply of ashes from a fireplace or wood stove.

4 tablespoons baking soda
2 cups wood ashes

Mix well and store in closed container. To use, mix a portion with just enough water to form a paste. Rub on with a damp sponge or soft cloth. Rinse and dry.

ELECTROLYTIC SILVER CLEANER

A quick way to clean tarnished sterling silver or silver plated pieces en masse without resorting to chemical or abrasive polishing one piece at a time is to remove the black silver sulfide tarnish "electrically." This is not for cemented pieces like hollow-ware or pieces with an oxidized or French finish. Place a piece of aluminum foil in the bottom of a large non-aluminum pan or the kitchen sink. Add a boiling solution of 1 tablespoon baking soda or 1 teaspoon baking soda plus 1 teaspoon salt per quart of water. Immerse the silver, making sure there is enough hot solution to completely cover it. With the silver in contact with the aluminum, an electric cell is formed causing the silver sulfide to dissolve. The dissolved silver is separated from the sulfur and redeposited on the solid pieces. After a few minutes the silver pieces should be tarnish-free. If not, the process can be repeated with fresh solution. This process will remove the dark accents in design crevices, which you may or may not like. The freshly cleaned silver should be thoroughly rinsed and then buffed dry with a soft cloth. This process will leave a somewhat duller luster than a regular polish. If you prefer a high shine and don't mind polishing each piece individually, the electrolytic method can be used to remove the tarnish from a number of pieces at once, which can then be polished to a high shine one at a time with a commercial polish.

VERDIGRIS REMOVER

Unlacquered copper easily forms the green tarnish of toxic copper carbonate known as verdigris. This is why copper pans are often lined with other metals like stainless steel, chromium and tin. On solid copper cookware, verdigris will form from reaction with certain acidic foods. Verdigris can be removed from unlacquered copper, and unlacquered brass and bronze (both alloys of copper) as well, with a paste made from one tablespoon baking soda and one tablespoon deodorized kerosene (from the hardware store). After scouring, rinse well and dry.

COPPER/BRASS BRIGHTENER

Unlacquered copper and brass can be cleaned and brightened by applying a paste of baking soda and lemon juice. Rub on and leave for a few minutes. Then rinse well with warm water, and dry.

BRASS LACQUER REMOVER

Most decorative brass produced in recent years has been sold with a protective lacquer coating to keep it bright and shiny without the need for polishing. In fact, cleaners and polishes should not be used on lacquered items, just a dust cloth and occasional damp sponge. If the lacquer cracks and peels it has to be removed and the item has to be relacquered (you can buy the spray at the hardware store). To remove peeling lacquer from brass, submerge the item in a bucket containing a solution of ½ cup baking soda for each gallon of boiling water. Leave the item in the solution until it cools to room temperature. You should then be able to just peel the lacquer off.

ALUMINUM CLEANER

Aluminum screens, doors and furniture, whether painted or unpainted, can be cleaned with a solution of ¼ cup baking soda per gallon of warm water. Cleaned painted aluminum will benefit from a periodic coating of low or no abrasive automobile wax.

Sports Equipment Cleaner
Plastic, fiberglass and aluminum sporting equipment can be cleaned with a paste of three parts baking soda for each part water. This will remove most spots and stains, and can be followed by washing with a mild detergent, rinsing and drying.

Running Shoe Deodorant
The odor of running shoes, and other athletic footwear, can be controlled between uses by sprinkling in two to four tablespoons of baking soda and distributing over the entire insole.

Book Deodorant
If a treasured book has picked up a musty smell from damp basement storage or after having been wet, first make sure the book is totally dry. Then sprinkle a little baking soda between the pages and leave it there several days before brushing it out.

Play Clay
When you're through cleaning with baking soda, play with it.

2 cups baking soda
1 cup cornstarch
1¼ cups cold water
Food coloring, as desired

In a saucepan, blend the baking soda and cornstarch. Add the water, with any food coloring desired, and cook over medium heat, stirring constantly. When the mixture is the consistency of mashed potatoes, turn out on a plate and cover with a damp cloth. When cool enough to handle, it is ready to use. Objects made from this clay are best air dried for 24 hours; thick pieces may take longer. The drying of thin pieces can be accelerated by placing in a preheated 350° oven for 15 minutes. Too-rapid drying of thin objects or oven drying of thicker objects can result in cracking. Dried pieces can be painted with water colors, poster paints or felt tip pens, and then coated with shellac, varnish, liquid plastic or nail polish. Unused clay can be stored in a tightly sealed plastic bag in the refrigerator, but should warm to room temperature before use.

Stalagmites & Stalactites
In underground caves, minerals dissolved in slowly dripping water form stalactites (growing down from the ceiling) and stalagmites (seemingly growing up from the ground). This process can be easily demonstrated using baking soda and a few simple props:

6 teaspoons baking soda
hot water
2 small glass baby food size jars
1 large flat disposable plastic plate
household glue
14 inch piece of wool yarn

Glue the two jars to the plate about four inches apart. Fill the jars with hot water and dissolve three teaspoons of baking soda in each. Put the ends of the yarn in the solution in each jar, allowing the middle to hang between the jars while remaining at least ½ inch above the plate. After sitting undisturbed for two or three days, stalactites will have formed on the yarn and stalagmites beneath it. This happens because the baking soda solution travels up the yarn and drips onto the plate. The drops on the plate evaporate, leaving behind a stalagmite of baking soda. Water evaporating from the solution absorbed in the yarn leaves behind stalactites of baking soda.

Poor Man's Plaster
To temporarily fill cracks in plaster, add just enough white craft glue to baking soda to make a paste. Work this into the crack

with your finger making the surface as smooth as possible.

Cookout Flame Extinguisher

When you barbeque meat, fat dripping on hot coals can cause flames to shoot up to the food. To control this, put a solution of one teaspoon baking soda in one pint of water into a plastic spray bottle. Spray it at the base of the flames as needed; it's more effective than water alone. This can also be brought on camping trips to ensure that the campfire is completely extinguished.

Pool Water Stabilizer

The pH and alkalinity of swimming pool water should be controlled to maintain water clarity, provide optimum disinfection by the chlorine, and to avoid eye sting. Baking soda is an effective alternative to the chemicals sold in pool supply stores to adjust alkalinity and pH. At the beginning of the season, if the pool water is below the minimum acceptable pH of 7.2, add 3 to 4 lbs. of baking soda for every 10,000 gallons of water. Check the pH every week. If the pH is at least 7.2 but below 7.5 - a condition where eye irritation and burning can be a problem - add 2 lbs. of baking soda for each 10,000 gallons of water to raise the pH. To prevent clouding, especially in hard water areas or when using a calcium chlorinating agent, keep the pH below 7.8. In order to control pH without fluctuation, adequate alkalinity should be maintained. Alkalinity should be kept in the 110 to 150 ppm range for stabilized chlorinated isocyanurates, and 60 to 110 ppm for other chlorinating agents. Each 1½ lbs. of baking soda adds 10 ppm alkalinity for every 10,000 gallons of water.

Potting Soil Alkalizer

To flourish, some potted plants prefer an alkaline soil. Home gardeners can raise the pH of potting soil safely with a solution of four tablespoons baking soda per quart of water. (Soil for acid loving plants can be adjusted with a solution of four tablespoons powdered alum per quart of water.) This should not be used as a routine treatment. A high accumulation of sodium salts in the soil will be harmful to some plants.

Garden Fungicide
As a nontoxic alternative to chemical fungicides, a solution of four teaspoons baking soda per gallon of water sprayed on rose bushes will help prevent damage by black spot fungus. Adding a few drops of liquid soap to the solution will help it spread more evenly on the leaves.

This same spray can be used on grapes and vines to help prevent grape fungi, especially black rot, from forming. Apply once when the fruit starts to appear and then once a week for about two months; reapply after each rain.

Garden Greener
To green up garden plants and bushes, try the following.

1 teaspoon baking soda
1 teaspoon Epsom salts
½ teaspoon clear ammonia
1 gallon water

Mix well and store in an airtight container. Apply at rate of about one quart per rose bush size shrub.

Roach Killer
Probably the safest (to humans) preparation claimed to kill roaches and silverfish is a blend of equal parts baking soda and sugar. The sugar will get them to eat it and the large amount of baking soda they will consume in relation to their weight is supposed to kill them. Just spread the powder near infested areas. Although this blend is innocuous to warm blooded species, it is best to keep children and pets away from it as you would any insect poison.

BAKING SODA IN THE GARAGE

Baking soda can be used in a number of ways to keep your car, motorcycle, boat and the garage in which they're kept looking good.

Windshield and Chrome Cleaner
To remove dead bugs, sap, bird droppings, tar and traffic grime from chrome, windshields and headlights, scrub with baking soda on a damp sponge and wipe with a paper towel. If a little more power is needed, try the following:

ALL-PURPOSE CLEANER
¼ cup baking soda
1 cup clear ammonia
½ cup white vinegar
1 gallon warm water

Mix well. Use rubber gloves and maintain adequate ventilation. Wipe on cleaner with a paper towel, let dry to a powdery haze, and wipe off with a clean paper towel. Use a nylon scrubber for careful spot scrubbing if necessary.

Vinyl and Canvas Cleaners
A solution of four tablespoons baking soda per quart of water or baking soda sprinkled on a damp sponge will remove oils and grease that can embrittle vinyl seating. Follow with a clear water rinse and wipe dry.

To remove tree sap, bird droppings and general traffic grime from vinyl tops and canvas convertible car and boat tops, scrub with a paste of three parts baking soda per part of water and a soft bristle scrub brush. Follow with a mild detergent wash, rinse well and dry.

Auto/ Boat Deodorizer
If your car or boat suffers from lingering odors from smoke, mildew, and sick or incontinent children or pets, sprinkle baking soda liberally on all dry carpeting and cloth upholstery surfaces. Leave on overnight if possible and then vacuum. Then wash all nonabsorbent surfaces with a solution of four tablespoons baking soda per quart of water, rinse and dry.

Cover the bottom of ashtrays with baking soda to control smoke odors and to quickly extinguish smoldering butts.

Auto Floor Cleaners
When you are ready to vacuum out the latest accumulation of sand and dirt from your car's carpeting, first make sure it is dry and then spinkle liberally with baking soda. Let sit for 15 minutes and them vacuum. It will come cleaner and smell better.

Oily and greasy stains on auto carpeting (and cloth upholstery) can be absorbed with equal parts baking soda and salt or cleaned with a paste of three parts baking soda per one part water. Sprinkle the powder on the stain, brush lightly, leave for a few hours and then vacuum. Rub the paste into the stain, let dry, and then brush or vacuum away.

For carpeting that is musty and mildewy from having been wet, dry thoroughly first and then sprinkle baking soda liberally beneath (if it can be lifted) and on top and let sit overnight before vacuuming. Repeat if necessary.

Nautical Brass Cleaners
Unlacquered brass fittings on boats can be cleaned and brightened by applying a paste of baking soda and lemon juice. Rub on and leave for a few minutes. Then rinse well with warm water and dry.

Fittings of unlacquered brass (an alloy containing copper) can form the green tarnish of copper carbonate known as verdigris. Verdigris can be removed from brass with a paste made from one tablespoon baking soda and one tablespoon deodorized kerosene. After scouring, rinse well and dry.

Fiberglass Body Cleaner
Stains and grime on fiberglass car and boat body panels can be safely cleaned by scrubbing with baking soda on a damp sponge, followed by rinsing and drying. For extra tough stains, try leaving the wet baking soda after scrubbing until it dries and then wiping the powder away.

Garage Floor Spotter
Baking soda alone, and in combination with mason's sand, cornmeal, cat litter or diatomaceous earth (from your pool supply dealer), can be used to absorb spilled oil and grease from the garage floor. For the really finicky, any leftover stain can be cleaned by wetting the area and scouring with baking soda and a scrub brush.

Battery Terminal Cleaner
Corroded battery posts and cable connectors can be easily cleaned with a paste of three parts baking soda per one part water. After cleaning and drying, coat with a small amount of petroleum jelly.

Auto & Boat Fire Extinguisher
Keep a large box of baking soda handy in the car, boat and garage for extinguishing small oil, gas and engine fires. From a safe distance, broadcast the baking soda at the base of the flames. If the fire is too large or intense to respond quickly to the baking soda, call the fire department immediately.

Engine Degreaser
You can mix your own degreasing compound for use as needed

by just mixing with water. The following blend will let you avoid cleaners containing volatile and flammable solvents. The ingredients other than baking soda can be obtained at a hardware store; they are skin irritants so be sure to wear eye protection and rubber gloves when mixing and using.

ENGINE DEGREASER

1 cup baking soda
½ cup sodium metasilicate
3 cups trisodium phosphate

Mix well and store in a well sealed container. To use, mix ½ to 1 cup with enough water to form a spreadable paste. Scrub on with a stiff brush, wait for 10 to 15 minutes and rinse.

BAKING SODA FOR PERSONAL CARE

Shampoo
When your hair is suffering from dandruff or conditioner overload, try getting it back to its natural state without the commercial formulated concoctions. Instead of shampooing, wet your hair and vigorously rub in a handful of baking soda. Be sure to massage it into your scalp as well. Rinse thoroughly and air dry if possible or blow dry at the coolest setting that will get the job done. Your hair might look dry at first, but with regular washing (which should be no less frequent than every other day if you have a dandruff problem) with baking soda, dandruff should diminish and your hair should become naturally soft. Once your hair and scalp have returned to a naturally healthy state, alternate washings with baking soda and baby shampoo.

Anti-Chlorine Hair Rinse
Over-chlorinated pool water can leave hair dull or discolored. Counteract chlorine's effects by rinsing your hair with a solution of one half teaspoon baking soda per pint of water.

Eye Relief
For relief from smoke or pollution irritated eyes, use an eye wash cup or sterile eye dropper to apply a solution of a scant ⅛ teaspoon of baking soda per cup of sterile water. Make fresh solution as needed.

Contact Lense Storage Fluid
The following solution can be tried for storing hard contact lenses between wearings.

HARD CONTACT LENSE FLUID
¼ teaspoon baking soda
¼ teaspoon salt
1 cup sterile water

Mix well in a sterile container until the baking soda and salt are dissolved. Pour the solution through a paper coffee filter to remove any undissolved particles and store in a sterile dropper bottle.

Earwax Softener
If you are bothered by excessive buildup of hardened earwax, try a few drops of this softener at bed time.

EARWAX SOFTENER
¼ teaspoon baking soda
½ cup glycerine (from the pharmacy)
1 cup sterile water

Mix well in a sterile container until clear. Store in a sterile dropper bottle.

Mouthwash/ Gargle
Rinsing or gargling with a solution of one teaspoon baking soda in a half glass of water will be as effective as most minty and medicated commercial preparations.

Teeth/ Gum Cleaners
As the ever increasing popularity of commercial baking soda toothpastes indicates, baking soda is a safe and effective way to keep your teeth and gums clean and healthy. A little baking soda on a wet toothbrush provides all the cleaning and polishing action necessary while deodorizing and neutralizing acidic bacterial wastes.

Some people do not care for the taste of baking soda alone and add a drop or two of flavoring oils or extracts. Some prefer a paste of baking soda and mashed strawberries, which are supposed to have dental stain removing properties of their own.

For extra whitening and antibacterial action, brush with a paste of baking soda and hydrogen peroxide, paying extra attention to cleaning at the gum line.

Denture Cleaner
Dentures can be soaked in a solution of four tablespoons baking soda per quart of water and scrubbed with baking soda on a wet toothbrush.

Canker Sore Relief
Canker sores are a result of viral infection, but it is an overlying bacterial infection which causes the painful whitish sore. The bacteria and their secretions are acidic and can be neutralized by swishing a solution of one teaspoon baking soda in half a glass of warm water gently through your mouth. This will help relieve the pain.

Preshave/ Aftershave
For those with sensitive skin, a solution of one tablespoon baking soda per cup of water makes a soothing preshave or aftershave splash that can minimize irritating razor burns.

Blackheads Treatment

To loosen blackheads, mix equal parts baking soda and water and apply. Rub gently for two or three minutes, then rinse with very warm water. Do not squeeze.

Leg Shaving Aid

A solution of one tablespoon baking soda per cup of water is an alternative to shaving cream or soap and water for shaving your legs with a safety razor.

Foot Bath

A periodic ten minute soak in a solution of four tablespoons baking soda per quart of warm water will relieve tired feet, soften calluses, and relieve athlete's foot itching.

Athlete's Foot Care

Athlete's foot is caused by fungi and yeast that can proliferate in the hot sweaty environment in shoes. The best prevention is to keep feet dry by wearing absorbent socks and correctly fitting shoes that are made of breathable material like leather. A light dusting of baking soda on the feet will help reduce moisture from perspiration and in hot and humid weather can be supplemented with a foot soak in baking soda solution (see above). If you have athlete's foot, rub the affected area, especially between toes, with baking soda to which just enough tepid water has been added to form a paste. Rinse, dry thoroughly and apply an over-the-counter athlete's foot treatment.

Foot Smoother

Hard and rough areas on the feet, such as heels and calluses, can be smoothed and softened by a massage with a paste of three parts baking soda per one part water. Follow with a baking soda solution foot bath (see above), rinse and dry thoroughly.

Nail Care

Toe and finger nails can be kept clean by scrubbing with a wet nail brush dipped into baking soda. This will soften cuticles too.

Bath Salts

There is little to rival the relaxing effect of soaking in a hot bath, especially after working, exercising or playing hard. While you're soaking, a half cup of baking soda dissolved in the bath water will clean away dirt and perspiration, and neutralize body odors. The extra pampered, or extra sore, can try the following:

BUBBLING BATH SALTS

2½ cups baking soda
2 cups cream of tartar
½ cup cornstarch

Mix well and store in a covered container. A few drops of perfume can be blended in also if desired. Use a quarter cup per bathful.

RHEUMATIC BATH SALTS

2 cups baking soda
1 cup epsom salt (magnesium sulfate)
½ cup salt

Mix well and store in a covered container. Use a half cup per bathful.

Sponge Bath

When there's no time for a shower or bath, you can freshen up with a quick sponge bath using a solution of four tablespoons baking soda per quart of water. This will neutralize odors and wash away dirt and perspiration.

Knee and Elbow Scrub
While bathing children after a busy day outdoors, scrub grimy dirt from elbows and knees with baking soda sprinkled on a damp washcloth.

Deodorant
A natural alternative to deodorant sprays and lotions is to simply dust some baking soda under your arms to absorb perspiration and neutralize odors. This will save your clothes from deodorant stains as well.

Burns and Rashes
Generalized minor burns and rashes, like sunburn and prickly heat, can be relieved by soaking in a tepid bath containing one cup of baking soda. After soaking, do not rinse, just gently towel dry. If you haven't the time to soak, take a sponge bath using a solution of four tablespoons baking soda per quart of water.

More localized minor burns and rashes can be soothed with a wet compress of baking soda solution or a paste of three parts baking soda to one part water or witch hazel. Either baking soda paste will also help relieve the itch of poison ivy.

Sunburn blisters can be treated with a sterile dressing soaked in the baking soda solution.

Insect Bites and Stings
The pain and irritation of most common insect bites and stings can be relieved by quick application of baking soda mixed with just enough water, witch hazel or clear ammonia to form a paste. Keep the paste moist by covering with a damp cloth or dressing.

Antacids
The generations-old relief for acid indigestion and heartburn is

baking soda. Take a level half teaspoon dissolved in four fluid ounces of water.

For those spoiled by the convenience of prepared antacid liquids, try the following:

ANTACID LIQUID
1 tablespoon baking soda
1 teaspoon sugar
4 drops (to taste) peppermint oil
1 cup water

Mix well and store in an airtight bottle in the refrigerator. When needed, take one to two tablespoons.

Baking soda contains sodium. If you suffer from hypertension or are on a salt restricted diet, consult your health care professional before taking internally. While baking soda is a natural choice for neutralizing stomach acids, it is not a remedy for other types of stomach problems such as nausea, stomach ache, gas pains, abdominal cramps, or stomach distention (bloating) caused by overeating or overdrinking.

THREE

Baking,

Brushing
&
Bovines

Why do Elsie and Elmer use more baking soda than you or I?
(see page 105)

THREE

BAKING, BRUSHING & BOVINES

The evolution of baking soda's utility in the home has spawned a proliferation of uses on a commercial scale. Applications in countless consumer and industrial products and processes have developed throughout the 20th century. From dialysis to drilling muds, from foam rubber to fire extinguishers, its cleaning, polishing, neutralizing and gas liberating properties have made it the natural solution to diverse technical problems. The following are three prominent commercial uses of baking soda which serve as good examples of its unique versatility and effectiveness. Baking soda's contribution to better cakes and cleaner teeth are no secret. Few appreciate, however, how it promotes more milk and better beef.

BAKING WITH BAKING SODA

As described in Section 1, baking soda's first widespread use was as a leavening agent. Leavening is simply the act of introducing gas bubbles into a dough or batter so that it expands. The three basic approaches to leavening are generation of carbon dioxide by the reaction of baking soda with an acid, generation of carbon dioxide by fermentation of yeast, and mechanical incorporation of air by whipping or beating.

A general rule of thumb is that soda leavens batters while yeast leavens dough. There are, of course, exceptions. Yeast produces carbon dioxide fairly slowly so it requires a reasonably strong and elastic matrix to contain the generated gas. A relatively stiff, gluten-containing dough is needed. Batters and weak doughs do not benefit from yeast leavening because there is no means to contain the liberated gas. Most of the carbon dioxide would exit the mixture as it was produced. This type of composition needs a relatively fast acting gas source, one that will aerate the batter or dough quickly, but not so quickly that it will collapse during baking once the leavening period is over. In the past century and a half, no more suitable product than baking soda has been found. Baking soda can liberate carbon dioxide at a controlled rate; it is inexpensive, highly purified, and nontoxic.

Baking soda is used as the sole leavening agent if the dough or batter contains a naturally acidic ingredient to react with it. This is the case when sour milk, buttermilk, yogurt, molasses, chocolate, or fruit preserves are used. Commercial baking powders are made from a combination of sodium bicarbonate with one or more acid ingredients and an inert powder like starch to control moisture absorption and prevent premature reaction. The starch also allows adjustment of the baking soda content to approximately 30% in most baking powders, since the several acids each require inclusion at a different ratio with the baking soda to ensure proper reaction.

There is a host of baking acids used with baking soda in household baking powders and in food industry preparations. These include cream of tartar, tartaric acid, monocalcium phosphate, sodium aluminum sulfate, sodium aluminum phosphate, sodium acid pyrophosphate, dicalcium phosphate dihydrate, and glucono delta-lactone. Historically, the first baking powders were blends of baking soda with cream of tartar. This combination reacts very quickly so that a batter had to be quickly mixed and put into the oven before the gas evolution was spent. This type of prepared baking powder was succeeded by Professor Horsford's double acting blend, still current, using monocalcium phosphate in place of cream of tartar. The phosphate reacts somewhat slower than the tartrate so that about two thirds of the carbon dioxide is liberated during mixing of the batter or dough, and the rest only in response to the heat of the oven. Another of the baking powders sold today for home use contains both monocalcium phosphate and sodium aluminum sulfate. This powder releases about one third of its carbon dioxide during mixing and two thirds during baking.

Baking powder use in the home was most prevalent prior to World War II. Since then, the availability of commercial baked goods and prepared mixes has concentrated demand among those who remain unintimidated by the concept of "scratch" baking. Also during this time period, growth and sophistication in the prepared foods industry has promoted the preference for separate purchase of baking soda and baking acid to fine tune the leavening and finished properties of each particular baked good. Although a steady market for preblended baking powders still exists in both the home and the food industry, three quarters or better of the soda/acid leavening used in the U.S. is by user blending of baking soda with the preferred baking acid for the job. In the home, many bakers prefer to use baking soda with cream of tartar or one of the acidic foods previously noted. Baking soda is also used together with baking powder in certain recipes. Although this might seem redundant, the added baking soda is used to provide leavening action sooner and to a greater degree than what would occur with the baking powder alone. The extra baking soda can also be used to promote surface browning and flavor development since the distinctive flavor compounds generated in many baked goods are formed in the outer surfaces and diffuse inward on cooling.

Producers of commercial baked goods or baking mixes have a choice among the baking acids. The particular combinations with baking soda are chosen based on considerable research into their effects on the finished product. The soda/acid leaven not only produces carbon dioxide, it determines the final texture of the baked or cooked food and indirectly affects the flavor, moisture and general palatability.

For example, sodium aluminum phosphate is used in consumer cake mixes because it has a great tolerance to variations in mixing time, liquid level and oven temperature. This makes for a decent cake, no matter how inexperienced the home baker. Refrigerated tubed biscuit, muffin and roll doughs require the slow, controlled leavening obtained with the use of sodium acid pyrophosphate as the baking acid. Essentially no leavening is desired during mixing and tubing. The release of carbon dioxide then occurs within one day, eliminating any air pockets between dough and tube. This also promotes the formation of small gas bubbles in the dough from the pressure exerted by the dough trying to expand under confinement (this pressure is what causes the tube to pop open when the seal is broken). The small gas bubbles expand during baking to yield the raised finished baked product. Glucono delta-lactone is used as the baking acid in some tubed pizza and bread doughs because the nature of its reaction with baking soda provides results more closely resembling yeast leavening.

DENTAL CARE

Your grandmother brushed her teeth with baking soda, and her grandmother probably did as well. They were likely as disinterested in why it cleaned teeth as they were in a technical explanation of why it relieved acid indigestion or made their muffins rise. The essential point was that it worked. Non-food folk uses of common kitchen staples like vinegar, salt and baking soda have often depended as much on tradition as on efficacy for their perpetuation. The folk uses of baking soda are perhaps unique in that they have attracted the interest of the scientific community, which has invariably provided the scientific underpinnings for what grandma knew all along. Farmers were feeding their cows baking soda well before the scientific substantiation and economic advantages of this practice were documented. Housewives were using baking soda as a refrigerator deodorant a generation before its mechanism of action was defined. People were keeping their teeth clean and healthy with baking soda for more than 100 years before scientists affirmed that this was a good idea.

Baking soda offers a compelling collection of attributes as a dentifrice. It cleans and polishes, of course, but in the process it also reduces plaque and tartar buildup, deodorizes the mouth and leaves a particularly clean feeling. Baking soda is the only product in dental use today that was on the original list of products accepted by the American Dental Association in April, 1931. Its main drawbacks, however, have been the inconvenient powder form, the salty taste and the lack of cavity fighting fluoride. The first attempt to address these issues came in 1974 with the introduction of Peak® toothpaste by Colgate-Palmolive. Company promotion and consumer interest in this dentifrice, a product before its time, remained low for years. In 1986, sensing the growing interest in things natural, Church and Dwight, the baking soda experts (Arm & Hammer), began regional introduction of Dental Care® baking soda toothpaste with fluoride. Dental Care was available nationwide by 1988 and from the first has exceeded all sales expectations. This spawned a whole new catagory of dentifrice sales. Today, baking soda toothpastes are offered by every major dentifrice producer, and many smaller ones. This new toothpaste category accounts for about 10% of the $1.4 billion dentifrice market, and it's still growing.

While the scientific nod to the use of baking soda in toothpaste came decades after its folk use was well established, a related use of baking soda in dental hygiene derived from solid research. In the 1950's, Dr. Paul Keyes, D.D.S., a research scientist at the National Institute of Health, was already well known for demonstrating that certain bacteria are the cause of cavities. He decided to next investigate the cause of periodontal (gum) disease. Gum disease was then treated, and still is, by surgery, and in some cases, extraction. The gums are cut back to expose the infected pockets so they can be more thoroughly cleaned while brushing. Dr. Keyes discovered that it was severe bacterial infection beneath the gum line which causes the destructive degeneration of the root-membrane that leads to the loosening of teeth.

Dr. Keyes suggested that surgery needn't be the only, and certainly not the first, measure in the treatment of periodontal disease. He recommended a more conservative approach to treatment and prevention based on a combination of regular professional attention and conscientious home care. The latter included flossing and brushing, with particular attention paid to brushing at and below the gum line in order to remove bacterial plaque. It's this plaque which forms the breeding ground for the bacteria responsible for gum disease.

Plaque is a colorless, sticky, bacteria-laden film that coats the teeth, particularly along the gumline. If not removed, plaque accumulates and hardens into tartar. Plaque and tartar often remain undetected and undisturbed below the gumline, resulting in both tooth decay and gum disease. The bacteria in plaque thrive on sugar, converting it into acids that attack the tooth's enamel surface. Unchecked, this decay reaches the inner tooth, killing nerves and blood vessels and ultimately the tooth itself. Besides causing tooth decay, plaque and tartar below the gumline can separate the gums from the teeth. The gums become swollen and bleed easily. Without attention, the gums eventually pull away from the teeth and form pockets that collect food and infectious bacteria. Teeth can loosen and fall out.

The first step in the Keyes technique is for the dentist to collect a plaque sample from below the gum line and examine it under a microscope. Under magnification, the bacteria responsible for gum disease can be differentiated from the normal plaque microorganisms. The disease-causing bacteria are not found under healthy gums and so are readily identified and targeted for elimination. The treatment program is dentist supervised, but based on the patient's commitment to carefully follow a simple bacteria-fighting procedure.

After flossing and brushing tooth surfaces above the gum line, home care requires delivering a paste of baking soda and hydrogen peroxide beneath the gum line by holding the bristles of the toothbrush at an angle to the gum line when brushing, and by using a rubber-tipped probe to push the paste into each diseased pocket. The gum line is then rinsed with a solution of table salt in warm water. Dr. Keyes considered these ingredients - baking soda, peroxide and salt - mild bactericides which would be safe and effective for home use.

The patient visits the dentist at regular intervals so that the effectiveness of the procedure can be monitored by microscopic examination of the plaque bacteria, and modified as necessary. Once the bacterial infection is controlled, gum tissues begin to rejuvenate, and the frequency of visits to the dentist is reduced. The regimen of careful daily home care must be maintained, however, in order to avoid a recurrence of the disease.

This dental health management system is based on close professional supervision and good patient compliance so that the simple treatment with baking soda, hydrogen peroxide and salt can kill the disease-causing bacteria. It is only when the disease does not respond after eight or more months that surgery might be considered.

The Keyes system would seem to represent a more attractive

alternative than surgery or extraction, but it requires a dentist trained in the methodology, and a patient willing to make the repeat office visits and faithfully maintain the home treatment. Whether through the reluctance of periodontists or of patients, the widespread adoption of the Keyes system as the preferred treatment of gum disease has not occurred, although it is still practiced by many dentists. Nevertheless, the sound scientific basis of Dr. Keyes' work was transformed into yet another folk use of baking soda. People began brushing their teeth with a paste of baking soda and hydrogen peroxide (some even added salt) believing that the peroxide would provide added cleaning and whitening, and unaware of the original intent and true value of the combination.

The first commercially viable dentifrice to incorporate the baking soda/peroxide combination came in 1985 with the test marketing of Periogene® by Noxell. A peroxide gel and baking soda paste were kept separated in a two chambered container. They were dispensed simultaneously onto the toothbrush and mixed while brushing. Periogene apparently could not gain sufficient consumer interest, however, to prevent its withdrawal from the market.

In 1991, Chesebrough-Ponds took advantage of the explosive growth in the baking soda toothpaste market to introduce Mentadent®. This baking soda/peroxide dentifrice shared the same two compartment dispenser concept as its unsuccessful predecessor, and this time it caught on. Mentadent has since carved a secure niche in the baking soda segment of the toothpaste market, and encouraged the introduction of at least three similar products by other manufacturers.

The postscript to about six generations of the safe and effective use of baking soda in dental care is the scientific corroboration over the past decade of what grandma knew all along. Baking soda has been verified as safe and nonirritating to all oral tissues - again less than startling news since it is a natural component of saliva. Baking soda reduces stains and plaque by its gentle nonabrasive polishing action. Because it has soft crystals, it removes material adhering to teeth without abrading dentin or enamel. Tests have actually shown that toothpastes with high levels (60-65%) of baking soda clean as well as toothpastes with conventional abrasives while showing much lower abrasion scores. The mild alkalinity of baking soda can also react with and remove substances that dull or stain teeth. More importantly, baking soda reduces decay by neutralizing plaque acids. By helping to control plaque, it likewise controls tartar. Scientists have even documented the ability of the leading baking soda toothpaste to eliminate bad breath from subjects fed cheeseburgers with onion and garlic. Not content, apparently, that all bases were covered, a follow-up study was conducted on subjects who each drank a can of warm beer and then smoked two unfiltered cigarettes. Baking soda prevailed.

NOT JUST CHICKEN FEED

Today's dairy cow is bred for unprecedented milk production. A typical high-producing cow can give 90 pounds (about 11 gallons) of milk per day. Top producers easily exceed 100 pounds per day. Genetics, however, is only the foundation of this impressive output. A modern dairy cow is truly a milk factory. Genetics determines maximum productivity, but energy input dictates actual results. Energy comes in the form of food, which is broken down by bacteria in the rumen (the partially digested food) and ultimately converted to milk. These rumen bacteria function at peak efficiency only in a fairly narrow pH range, between about pH 6.2 and pH 6.8.

Dairy cows eat a range of feedstuffs, from relatively low energy, high fiber food like dry hay and dry grass, to higher energy and more easily digestible silage (e.g. fermented chopped corn stalks) and fresh grass, to high energy grains. Maximum milk production and milk fat content depend on a substantial level of the high energy grain in the cow's diet. But these high grain, low fiber feeds require less chewing, which decreases saliva production. Since saliva contains naturally occurring sodium bicarbonate, less chewing and more grain cause rumen pH to drop below the optimum range. The more acidic the rumen, the less efficient its digesting bacteria become. When the bacteria becomes seriously inhibited, digestion slows, feed intake decreases, and milk production drops.

Not surprisingly, acid stomach in cows is readily corrected by supplementing saliva sodium bicarbonate with baking soda blended right into the high energy feed. This ensures that rumen pH is maintained in the proper range so the cow maintains optimum output.

A similar situation exists with beef cattle. When it is time to prepare the steer for market, they are put on a high energy, low fiber diet to maximize weight gain. Since this gain can average 100 pounds per month, and the rancher is paid per pound, the efficiency of food conversion is very important. As with his distaff counterpart, the steer produces less bicarbonate-containing saliva with the easier to chew, high grain, high energy feed. As his rumen pH drops, feed intake, feed efficiency and weight gain are reduced. Sodium bicarbonate addition to his feed prevents this, allowing the steer to gain weight faster and be ready for market sooner.

The success of sodium bicarbonate supplementation of high energy cattle feed has made this its single largest use in North America. Animal feed accounts for 26% of the 400-450,000 tons of sodium bicarbonate currently sold annually in the U.S. and Canada. This dwarfs the 16% used by the food industry, the next largest consumer, and the 10% each consumed by the two other major uses - pharmaceuticals and water treatment. This success has, in fact, attracted the attention of other livestock breeders, who are adopting the use of sodium bicarbonate to maximize the health and economic value of their animals.

Of course, baking soda is not limited to supporting our meat and milk supply. In chicken feeds, baking soda has shown the ability to promote tougher eggshells so that breakage between the hen house and your house is minimized.

THE FUTURE

The food (both human and animal) and oral hygiene benefits described here, plus the well established pharmaceutical applications have an obvious immediate impact on our daily lives. They also account for the bulk of all sodium bicarbonate sold. The future of baking soda and our environment are likewise intertwined in ways designed to improve the quality of our air, our water and our lives.

The cow is of the bovine ilk;
One end is moo, the other milk.

Ogden Nash

FOUR

The

Environmental

Alternative

What do a dentist, the Statue of Liberty and an airplane have in common? (see page 123)

FOUR

THE ENVIRONMENTAL ALTERNATIVE

For generations, the utility of baking soda as a cleaner, deodorizer and antacid in the home has been well appreciated. In recent years, the unique versatility of baking soda has been applied to no less an undertaking than the cleaning, deodorizing and deacidifying of the environment. Baking soda combats acid rain as effectively as it curbs acid stomach. It is as safe in removing paint from an airliner as it is in polishing stains from your teeth. It is as effective in reducing lead in drinking water as it is in cleaning corrosion from a car battery. At a time when high tech environmental solutions bear assessment for their downside as well as their potential benefit, baking soda has earned the accolade in environmental management that has been its sustaining hallmark in the home for so long - it is safe, effective and economical. Faint praise it may seem, but a combination rare today.

MUNICIPAL WATER TREATMENT

A significant source of lead for human exposure is drinking water, with millions of Americans exposed to lead contaminated water every day. Detecting contamination is complicated by the fact that lead levels in drinking water can vary markedly between distribution systems in the same area, between houses supplied by the same system, between different types of taps, and at different times of day at a single tap.

Lead and other toxic metals enter drinking water that is corrosive to piping in the distribution system and the home. Corrosion occurs when the water is at low pH or contains an oxidizing agent, such as chlorinating compounds or even just dissolved oxygen. Under these conditions, metallic lead from lead pipes or solder can be leached into the water. In some parts of the country, acid rain and lack of natural carbonates in the ground produce potable water supplies that are "soft," with the low dissolved mineral content, low pH and low alkalinity that promotes lead leaching. Fortunately, the lead that is toxic when dissolved in the water can be easily inhibited from leaching into the water by reaction with sodium bicarbonate to form a coating that will actually protect the inside of water pipes from corrosion.

When acid rain water percolates through limestone subsoil it leaches calcium salts, primarily as carbonates. Water hardness is a measure of these dissolved calcium ions (plus certain other minerals) and is reported as calcium carbonate equivalents. Soft water is common in areas where acid rain percolates through acidic clay subsoils and remains relatively free of dissolved minerals. With low pH and low carbonate content, potable soft water supplies can carry high lead levels.

Corrosive water of this type can be simply and inexpensively treated with a combination of sodium bicarbonate, to raise the level of carbonate alkalinity, and sodium hydroxide, to raise the pH. Under these conditions, lead and dissolved carbonate will react and form a durable, impermeable coating of lead carbonate (cerussite) and lead hydroxycarbonate (hydrocerussite) inside pipes that will protect against leaching of lead and other metals.

The most dramatic demonstration of the effectiveness of this approach was descibed in the Environmental Protection Agency newsletter, "CEM Message" of February 28, 1990.

"EPA guidelines governing drinking water quality have been published as "interim standards" for many years, however, it was not until the last decade that mandatory compliance became tied to numerical values. The Safe Drinking Water Act (SDWA) approved by Congress in 1974 and amended in 1986, called for the EPA to establish maximum contaminant levels (MCLs) for 88 specific chemicals and establish a timetable for action on toxic contaminants.

Final SDWA standards, expected early next year, will bring to 61 the number of contaminants affected. It will be no surprise to municipal water suppliers when the proposed ten-fold MCL reduction of lead - from .05 to .005 mg/L at the plant - becomes law. While there are some "non-action" contingencies in EPA's proposal, the new regulations are bound to trouble distributors in regions of the U.S. where excessive lead levels at the tap are largely a result of geological conditions at the source.

One of the affected regions is in New England, where acid rain and the lack of carbonate as natural limestone produce very soft water with low pH and alkalinity - a condition which favors corrosion of the distribution lines and consequent leaching of lead into drinking water. A 1977 study of 16 New England water distribution systems reported twelve of them exceeding the current lead standard of .05 mg/L, and the EPA itself found excess lead in over 90 percent of the samples collected in Vermont.

That same year, an OSHA team checking blood-levels of workers at a Bennington battery factory became alarmed when not only the workers, but a control group made up of other townspeople in this Vermont community, exhibited high lead content. The problem was traced to the town's corrosive water supply, and to the fact that one-third of the dwellings in Bennington had lead service lines connecting the water main to the houses. Lead levels as high as .86 mg/L were measured at the tap - *over 17 times the .05 mg/L maximum contaminant levels.*

The Vermont Department of Health and EPA's Region 1 office in Boston were alerted and immediately organized a survey of the Bennington area to evaluate possible quantitative effects of any future treatment scheme.

Beginning in April of 1977, three morning samples were collected at each of ten residential locations on a monthly basis. All the homes on the survey had lead service lines; most had interior copper plumbing.

While the pretreatment survey was in process, Bennington's Water Department heard a variety of proposals for solving the problem. The one that appeared most feasible, from the viewpoint of economy and implementation, was developed by Dr. James W. Patterson, Professor of Enviromental Engineering at Illinois Institute of Technology.

Patterson's technology was currently undergoing tests by two separate study groups working independently at the Institute and at the Lawrence Experiment Station in Massachusetts, both reporting favorable results. These groups were investigating the European corrosion control method of adjustment in pH in combination with the addition of sodium bicarbonate to reduce metal contaminants, a technique which although common in Europe, had never been applied specifically to limiting lead levels.

City officials agreed to test the bicarbonate method for raising the alkalinity to 20 mg/L. But owing to the extremely acidic condition of the untreated surface water (pH 4.9), it was necessary to also add small amounts of caustic to achieve a final pH of 8.0 to 8.6. Treatment was begun in June of 1977, allowing two months of pretreatment data to be evaluated.

...By the end of the month corrosion rates had dropped sharply. ...Within the first six months, lead corrosion was down by 92 percent, and copper by 85 percent. By January of 1978 average lead concentration had decreased from .21 to .021 mg/L - less than half of EPA's current MCL of .05.

...Heeding its [Town] manager's advice, the town gradually began replacing the offending lead pipes, giving top priority to those pipes serving households with young children.

Treatment has quietly continued over the past eleven years, with lead concentration levels maintained well within the current interim SDWA regulations.

...Bennington's water treatment costs are quite modest, considering that they have succeeded in overcoming a public health problem. ...the total cost for sodium bicarbonate and caustic amounts to about two cents per thousand gallons of water treated. Moreover, the present procedure obviates the need for more costly corrosion prevention chemicals, such as metaphosphates which are notorious for leaving sludges that run afoul of EPA waste-water regulations."

The success of the sodium bicarbonate/sodium hydroxide system in Bennington, Vermont has attracted the attention of other communities which depend on soft water for their potable supply. Since 1980, Fitchburg and Chicoppee, Massachusetts, Fort Collins, Colorado and Myrtle Beach, South Carolina have adopted sodium bicarbonate treatment for the control of lead in their drinking water. With the ever heightening concern over the problem of lead poisoning in children and the consequent progressive reduction by the EPA in permissible lead levels, sodium bicarbonate may well become a major weapon in the fight to keep the nation's water safe and potable.

ACID LAKE RECOVERY

Another side effect of acid rain, and perhaps one more widely known, is the formation of acid lakes. Most fish, and the aquatic organisms which feed them, thrive only in neutral pH water. Too much acidity, or for that matter too much alkalinity, is fatal. The unfortunate phenomenon of acid lakes is of primary concern in the Northeast U.S. and particularly in the Adirondack region of New York. As long as acid rain persists, acid lakes will remain a chronic problem which can be treated but not ultimately cured. Treatment, nevertheless, can be quite effective in reversing the mortality of at least small lakes where logistics and cost are not overwhelming. Not surprisingly, baking soda, the age old treatment for relieving stomach acid, is proving to be the most effective treatment for acid lakes as well.

The pH of surface waters (lakes, ponds, streams) is regulated by naturally present bicarbonate ion. In the 1950's, studies were conducted in Sweden which indicated that acidification of these waters proceeds in three steps. In the first, the natural alkalinity from the bicarbonate ion neutralizes the acid rain so that pH falls very slowly. Once the available bicarbonate is completely consumed, the addition of more acid rain causes a quick drop to below pH 5. The final stage is reached when the body of water stabilizes at pH 4.5 even with continued input of acid rain.

Liming has been used for some time to control the acidity of biologically stressed small lakes. Liming involves dumping cheap agricultural grade limestone (calcium carbonate) into the lake in quantities estimated to raise pH to the desired level. Liming, however, is an inexact and often inefficient process. Agricultural limestone is coarse and only slightly soluble in water. Up to two thirds of the amount added can be rendered totally ineffective by poor dissolution, rapid settling to the lake bottom, and occlusion by sediments and debris. In addition, a short term localized response as the limestone is added can be high alkalinity, in excess of pH 9. This can cause pH shock to organisms. Fine grinding of limestone increases its solubility and effectiveness somewhat, but elevates its cost as well.

Sodium bicarbonate has been proven as a safe and effective alternative to limestone for recovering acid waters. Sodium bicarbonate is completely and rapidly soluble and so is completely available for neutralizing acid. Due to its inherent nature as a pH buffer, it will not raise the pH over 8.2 even at high local concentrations before it is fully dispersed throughout the body of water. In effect, adding sodium bicarbonate is merely replacing the bicarbonate ion that naturally existed in the water prior to the influx of acid precipitation.

Although liming of lakes had been practiced with varying levels of success, a professor at Cornell University, James Bisogni, Jr., was the first to recognize and demonstrate the obvious advantages of sodium bicarbonate. In 1985 he adopted Wolf Pond, a 50 acre lake in the Adirondacks, as his laboratory. At the time, this lake had a pH of less than 5 and had been rendered essentially barren of game fish. Only a small number of trash fish survived. The simple addition of approximately 20 tons of an inexpensive grade of baking soda was successful in raising the pH and restoring the health of the lake.

After three years, the pH again began to decline due to seepage of lake water and acidic input from rain and ground water. A small addition of sodium bicarbonate restored the desired pH, allowing the lake to be stocked with trout for the summer season. The fish prospered and residents of the lake enjoyed good fishing once again. Since then, Dr. Bisogni has been successfully monitoring and maintaining the biological viability of Wolf Pond.

The use of sodium bicarbonate to revive acid lakes is an effective but limited expedient. It is a safe and reliable prescription for reviving and maintaining the health of relatively small lakes. It is probably an impractical approach to large bodies of water. It is not a cure, since the cause is the unavoidable influx of acidic water from acid rain and runoff. Fortunately, just as sodium bicarbonate can be used to remediate the adverse side effects of acid rain, it can be used to attack the causes of acid rain as well.

ACID RAIN RELIEF

Both coal and oil burning power plants produce acid gas emissions when the sulfur contained in the fuel is released up the flue stack in the form of sulfur dioxide (SO_2). This acid gas is ultimately returned to earth as acid rain. A major source of acid gas emissions is electric power generating plants. But when finely ground sodium bicarbonate is injected into the acidic flue gases of power plant boilers, it can remove over 90% of the sulfur dioxide contained. The sodium bicarbonate reacts with the sulfur dioxide to form solid salt cake (sodium sulfate) plus steam and carbon dioxide. The salt cake is collected in filter bags or in electrostatic precipitators along with the flyash. In fact, agglomeration of the flyash by the solid products of the bicarbonate reaction actually improves the collection of flyash and reduces the emission of particulates as well as sulfur dioxide from the smoke stack.

This dry injection of sodium bicarbonate is an alternative to the older technology using injection of lime slurries. In addition to improved efficiencies, the dry bicarbonate method is considerably less costly for equipment and maintenance, requires less space, uses no water, generates less solid waste, and is effective over a broader range of flue gas temperatures, up to 1200°F. While reduced power plant emissions are a considerable reward in and of themselves, the economies of operation offered by the use of sodium bicarbonate may even help to control the cost of electricity.

Large power plants were the initial target for injection of sodium carbonate, but its advantages on a smaller and even local scale have shown added potential for combating acid rain. Bicarbonate reduction of acid gas emissions from municipal waste incinerators and waste-to-energy facilities can be of particular benefit to local communities. Local and regional waste incinerators handle everything from common household

- 119 -

refuse to hospital wastes. The predominant acid gas from the combustion of solid waste is hydrogen chloride (HCl; hydrochloric acid), with lesser amounts of sulfur dioxide and other acid gases in relation to the nature of the waste incinerated. In reaction with sodium bicarbonate, the hydrogen chloride is converted to sodium chloride (NaCl; table salt) with liberation of steam and carbon dioxide. The dry injection of bicarbonate has been found to reduce HCl emisions up to 99% and total acid gas emissions up to 98%.

A dramatic example of the effectiveness of sodium bicarbonate in controlling acid emissions is the Southland Exchange-Joint Venture in Hampton, North Carolina. This regional facility burns up to 200 tons each day of solid waste. Serving hospitals along the Eastern seaboard, it is the largest incinerator of medical waste in the country with 30-40% of its daily input infectious or pathological waste. This facility began operation in 1986 with control solely on particulate emissions. After three years of operation, a sodium bicarbonate dry injection system was incorporated in reponse to regulatory pressure to reduce HCL emisions by 83% or to a level of 100 parts per million (ppm), whichever was lower. Just prior to the dry injection installation, HCL emissions while burning medical waste were more than six times the 100 ppm limit, and municipal waste incineration exceeded this figure more than fourfold.

As the product of waste incineration at 2200°F, the acid gases to be treated were at a temperature in excess of 500°F. The injection equipment was designed to contact the acid gas with sodium bicarbonate for all of three seconds. After installation, HCL emissions were cut by 98% on average, to only about one tenth of the permissible 100 ppm.

The added advantage of the bicarbonate method, as seen here, is the ability to be adopted as an affordable retrofit for facilities which were built with no provision for controlling acid gas.

This is a particular advantage for municipal waste incinerators, allowing the local government an affordable option in meeting air pollution control requirements.

DIOXIN DETERRENT

Flyash and acid gases are not the only emissions of concern from municipal waste burning facilities. The potential health effects of the dioxins produced in minute quantities in flue gases of waste-to-energy plants are also often an issue in the surrounding community. These chlorinated hydrocarbons form in the presence of flue gas HCl at high temperatures, around 600°F. This is before acid removal, which is generally accomplished after the gases have cooled somewhat. The dioxins are removed at the same time the acid gases are neutralized, but they end up in the flyash, creating a solid waste disposal problem. Baking soda has been proposed as a means of preventing the formation of dioxins and eliminating concern over their emission or disposal.

The unique advantage of sodium bicarbonate over other neutralizers is based upon its manner of heat decomposition. At flue gas temperatures, sodium bicarbonate particles resemble popping corn, giving off over one third of their weight as water and carbon dioxide as they "pop." As decomposition proceeds, the particles continually generate fresh reactive surfaces that become coated with the neutralization products, such as sodium chloride (from HCl) and sodium sulfate (from SO_2). Unlike other neutralizers, like lime, that become sealed in a coating of reaction products so that their unreacted interiors become unavailable, sodium bicarbonate is continually decomposing, "popping," and offering fresh surface for reaction with the acid gases.

Sodium bicarbonate not only offers the highest reaction rate and utilization efficiency of the available neutralizers, its efficiency actually increases at higher temperatures, with excellent HCl removal reported up to 1500°F. This makes the bicarbonate particularly well suited to injection into flue gases hotter than 600°. It holds promise for removing HCl before this acid can react with volatile organic chemicals to form chlorinated hydrocarbons. Dioxin formation could be prevented. An additional benefit is that at these temperatures toxic metals could also react with the bicarbonate to form insoluble salts, resulting in less toxic, unleachable flyash.

WASTE TREATMENT

The ability of sodium bicarbonate to react with and remove toxic metals is just one benefit of its use in municipal and industrial wastewater and sewage treatment plants. Its main function is maintaining proper pH and alkalinity to ensure proper biological control in waste digesters.

There are basically two processes by which bacteria are used to treat liquid wastes. Anaerobic (without oxygen) digestion uses bacteria that thrives in the absence of oxygen to reduce organic sludge and transform it into stable and easily dewatered residues. The drier and more compact these residues can be made, the less solid waste there is for disposal. Stabilization entails a two step biological conversion of organic solids to methane and carbon dioxide in airtight digesters. Aerobic (with oxygen) digestion uses bacteria which need oxygen to similarly feed on and convert organic wastes.

Both pH control and reserve alkalinity are important to the efficient operation of aerobic and anaerobic digesters. The breakdown of nitrogen-containing compounds depletes alkalinity, so that if sufficient bicarbonate levels are not maintained, volatile acids will form, reducing the pH and the conversion of organic solids. The solid residues will remain dispersed and difficult to dewater producing a wet sludge for disposal. The sodium bicarbonate keeps digesters running efficiently, aids in toxic metals removal, as noted, and of course provides odor control, especially of odiferous sulfides.

PAINT STRIPPING

Sodium bicarbonate's utility in keeping air and water clean has been further extended to a clever alternative to industrial-scale paint stripping that eliminates the need for hazardous chemical or mineral processes while minimizing the creation, and disposal costs, of hazardous coating wastes.

There have traditionally been two basic alternatives for stripping paint from large surfaces such as industrial equipment, metal superstructures and aircraft. Chemical strippers dissolve the coating through use of methylene chloride, phenols or sodium hydroxide. These chemicals constitute a disposal hazard by themselves, but once they also contain toxic metals like hexavalent chromium, lead and cadmium from the removed coating, the result is a chemical sludge that requires costly disposal as hazardous waste. Chemical strippers also pose a contact and inhalation danger to workers, who must use appropriate protective measures.

The alternative to chemical strippers has been sand blasting. This technique is fast, effective and economical, but can generate hazardous silica dust. Blasting with minute plastic beads instead of sand removes the threat of silicosis, but retains dust inhalation problems. All solid blast media, natural or man-made, tends to become contaminated with the coating it removes. If that coating contains hazardous components, all of the blasting media used must be considered hazardous waste and disposed of accordingly.

Thanks to experience in cleaning many teeth and one copper statue, there is an alternative to both hazardous chemicals and minerals in stripping paint. For some years, dentists have had the option of using the Prophy-Jet® instead of the more common abrasive paste and rotary polisher to clean teeth. This device can be used to direct a pressurized slurry of baking soda and water against the teeth to gently clean and polish. On a somewhat larger scale, a related technique was used in cleaning the tar coating from the inside of the delicate copper skin of the Statue of Liberty during its restoration. In this case, a compressor was used to direct a stream of dry bicarb for tar stripping. Sand blasting with baking soda in this way cleaned the copper without abrasion, and without exposing workers in the statue to hazardous blasting media.

With a bow to dentists and Lady Liberty, a blasting media has been developed that takes advantage of sodium bicarbonate's effective and safe cleaning properties. The use of baking soda in a water slurry is considered the safest, to workers and environment, and most effective alternative to the traditional paint stripping technologies. The slurry form minimizes dust generation and can be used on virtually all hard surfaces, including plastic composites. Because the bicarbonate-based media is water soluble, it is easily washed from the coating waste, which can then be concentrated for disposal. The separated bicarbonate solution can be sewered, if local regulations allow, or recovered for additional use as an acid neutralizer in treating electroplating wastes or supplying alkalinity to sewage treatment plants.

On industrial plant sites, the bicarbonate slurry method is preferred because it can be used to remove rust, corrosion and grease, in addition to coatings, and can be used safely on sensitive rotating and hard to reach equipment parts. Since the bicarbonate slurry does not cause sparking on metal surfaces (as sand can), does not leave gritty residues, and does not produce hazardous or flammable vapors, it can usually be used without interfering in normal plant operations.

The bicarbonate-based slurry method of paint removal has found growing acceptance in the aviation industry, where stripping paint from aircraft is vitally important to detect metal fatigue, cracks, corrosion, and other structural problems. Depainting aircraft has long depended on the use of methylene chloride-based strippers. Environmental and worker safety concerns in recent years spurred some movement towards dry blasting with plastic media. This, however, just traded one set of problems for another, since dust generation and ultimate disposal of larger quantities of solid hazardous wastes resulted. The plastic media also tended to fill minute cracks in the metal surfaces, masking stress defects it was supposed to uncover. It was also ineffective in removing corrosion or leaving a smooth, uncontaminated surface for repainting. The bicarbonate slurry approach has thus far successfully addressed all safety, efficacy, environmental and worker hygiene concerns while minimizing waste disposal problems. Quite a technological achievement, but probably no surprise to anyone who has ever used baking soda to remove stains from their teeth or burnt-on food from a casserole.

CARPET CONTROL

Release of volatile organic compounds is not only an issue affecting outdoor air quality. There is growing concern over the volatile organic compounds (VOCs) released from new building materials like plywood, pressboard and carpeting. Newer high energy efficiency office buildings and homes are heavily insulated to minimize the energy required for heating and cooling. Indoor air is recirculated, with relatively minor supplementation with fresh outdoor air. Volatile compounds can accumulate and produce adverse health effects. Symptoms from mild discomfort to illness have been attributed to volatile organics in confined, poorly ventilated spaces.

Broadloom carpeting is one prominent source of VOC

contamination of indoor air. The latex adhesives used to bind carpet tuft to the backing material contain volatile organics and generate additional volatile substances during the curing process. These substances include styrene, toluene and 4-PCH (4-phenylcyclohexene). Volatiles trapped in the finished carpet roll are released when the carpet is installed, creating the familiar "new carpet" smell. For most people this is an innocuous accompaniment to the new floorcovering. Some people, however, appear to be highly sensitive to these compounds.

At present, work is in the early stages in the development of a new sodium bicarbonate-based carpet treatment used during manufacture to significantly reduce the level of volatile organics released from carpeting. Cleaning and deodorizing soiled carpeting with baking soda has been a routine practice in the home for years. In the not too distant future, carpet manufacturers may use baking soda to deodorize their products right in the mill, ensuring safer and healthier indoor air.

FLUX FLUSHER

The many benefits of the electronic age have not been won without concern over environmental side effects. Even high tech ills, however, can be treated with a judicious dose of baking soda. In the production of electronic circuit boards, soldering flux residues have in the past been removed with chlorofluorocarbon solvents. The move away from ozone depleting chemicals, however, has presented certain challenges to the circuit board manufacturers. Soldering flux is generally one of two basic types - organic acid flux or rosin flux. The acid fluxes are water soluble, so removing residues can be managed with water alone. This is not effective on rosin-based flux. Saponifiers, usually highly alkaline chemicals, are therefore added to water to react with the rosin and make it water soluble for removal.

Typical saponifiers are quite caustic, at pH 12 to over 13, and can leach heavy metals from circuit board components; some also contain glycol ethers, which are water soluble organic solvents. These saponifiers can emit volatile organic compounds (VOCs) in use and produce waste water with relatively high Biological Oxygen Demand (BOD) and Chemical Oxygen Demand (COD).

Baking soda forms the basis of a new saponifier which avoids the problems associated with previous circuit board cleaners. This new saponifier is much less caustic than those commonly used, contains no VOCs, and is odorless. The baking soda reacts with the rosin flux in much the same way as it solubilizes grease and fats in kitchen cleaners. The circuit boards are cleaned, emissions into the air are eliminated, and waste water is low in BOD, COD and heavy metals.

SOIL SAVER

Baking soda's safety, efficacy and economy are not restricted to improving our air and water. They can be applied to the ground beneath us with equal benefit. Among the newest technologies to apply baking soda to an environmental problem is the treatment of contaminated soils. There are numerous sites in this country, and abroad, where the ground itself bears detectable levels of hazardous chemicals. Of great concern are the various halogenated (i.e. containing chlorine or bromine) organic chemicals which have seeped into the ground at manufacturing sites and landfills, as well as halogenated pesticides which have accumulated after application or which have been inadvertently liberated during manufacture or disposal.

Once an area of contaminated ground has been delineated, the standard treatment is either removal to a special hazardous waste landfill, or incineration. Transport to a designated landfill is not currently favored because it simply moves the hazard instead of eliminating it. Incineration is preferred since the chemical contaminants are effectively destroyed. While this would appear to be a straightforward approach, it is a logistical challenge and can be an economic nightmare. Once the extent of contamination has been determined, this entire volume of soil must be excavated and fed to the incinerator. Depending upon the amount and accessability of the soil to be treated, incineration may be done on-site. Otherwise, it must be shipped by secure transport to an appropriate facility. Incineration costs can be as much as $2000 per ton on-site and up to 50% greater off-site.

To provide some perspective, one ton of soil will fill a cube roughly four feet in each dimension. In other words, it can cost up to $3000 to burn the amount of dirt you could hide under your dining room table. On a more realistic scale, it can cost over $2 million to treat just the top twelve inches of an acre of land.

Various chemical means of rendering the halogenated contaminants non-hazardous have been tried in an effort to avoid the high cost of incineration. One promising approach has been to "cook" the soil with polyethylene glycol and a caustic like sodium hydroxide for four hours at 300°F. This, however, only partially degrades the contaminants and generates slightly toxic byproducts. Although 85-90% less costly than incineration, this method only reduces the contaminant level.

The U.S. Environmental Protection Agency, in conjunction with the Navy's Civil Engineering Lab, has in just the past few years developed a baking soda solution to this environmental problem. They have invented the Base-Catalyzed Decomposition (BCD) Process. This is an efficient, relatively inexpensive method for decomposing PCBs (polychlorinated biphenyls), pentachlorophenol (a wood preservative), polychlorinated dibenzo-p-dioxins, polychlorinated dibenzofurans, and halogenated pesticides like lindane, dieldrin and DDT. This process also minimizes air emissions and toxic residual wastes.

The BCD process involves crushing and screening the contaminated soil, and then blending in sodium bicarbonate at 10% of its weight. This blend is then heated for about one hour in a rotary reactor at 630°F. Under these conditions, the sodium bicarbonate strips the halogen from the chemical hazard and converts it to a simple salt. The resulting soil is nonhazardous and can be returned to the site of its excavation. This technology is suited to on-site cleanup, eliminating transportation costs. It is also the safest and most effective chemical method available, and can be implemented for only about 10% of the cost of incineration. Full scale tests of the BCD process are currently under way. They are expected to verify the technology and secure yet another application for baking soda in environmental management.

Never does nature say one thing
and wisdom another.

Juvenal

APPENDIX

Baking

&

Baking Soda

Will your freshly baked bread stale more quickly on the counter or in the refrigerator? (see page 150)

APPENDIX

BAKING & BAKING SODA

A book on baking soda would not be complete without recipes. Recipes by themselves, however, would be inconsistent with the objectives of this book. A full appreciation of how and why baking soda is used in baking is obtained only through an understanding of the common baking ingredients and how they work with baking soda to such delicious ends. There is a rhyme and reason to why baking soda leavened foods and yeast leavened foods have definite differences in taste and in the ingredients of success. As with most other of its major uses, the understanding of how best to use baking soda in baking was developed by generations of consumers using trial, talent and intuition. It has only been fairly recently that science has been able to supplement this empirical knowledge and thereby enhance the "art" of baking.

Most home baked goods are composed of relatively few ingredients, namely flour, leavening, salt, liquids (usually water or milk), eggs, shortening, and sweeteners. A basic understanding of how these ingredients interact in a batter or dough will help explain why baking soda, alone or as baking powder, is used in preference to yeast or mechanical leavening (i.e. simply whipping in air) in various items. For baking soda applications, the term baked will be used broadly to encompass pan fried foods like pancakes to deep fried foods like doughnuts and fritters. The common denominator among all these uses is flour as the major ingredient, and the need to develop a crumb, or porous texture to the finished product. Baking soda is used in certain baked goods for more than its leavening properties. In crackers, for example, it controls browning and neutralizes yeast by-products. Its major function, nevertheless, is to react with acids, liberate carbon dioxide, and control the raising, spreading and ultimate texture and palatability of cooked batters and doughs.

Since the main ingredient in most baked goods is flour, the characteristics of the most commonly used flours will form the scientific basis for the art of baking with baking soda.

FLOUR

Most home baking today is with wheat flour because wheat is the only edible grain that provides sufficient gluten when mixed with water to trap leavening gases and allow for a raised product. Gluten is the plastic and elastic product of the interaction of the grain's protein. Gluten is considered plastic because it will change its shape (stretch) under pressure, and elastic because it will resume its original shape when the pressure is removed. A wheat dough will, therefore, expand to incorporate the leavening carbon dioxide, air, or steam, but will be resistant to thinning to the point of rupture. Good gluten development is of obvious value in bread dough, but of lesser importance in cake and pastry doughs, or in batters. In general, the higher the wheat protein, the higher its gluten content when mixed into a dough. Also, the higher the protein content, the harder the wheat kernel.

Three basic types of wheat are grown in the U.S. today, differentiated by their hardness and consequent use in food. The bulk of the American wheat crop, approximately 75%, is hard wheat intended for bread baking. Hard wheat flour is low in starch, high in protein, and forms a strong gluten. Soft wheat, accounting for about 20% of the harvest, has a lower protein content, more starch, and develops a weak gluten. Soft wheat flours are preferred for cakes and soda/acid leavened products in general. The balance of the U.S. crop is the especially hard durum wheat. Durum gluten is very strong but not sufficiently elastic for general use in bread. Durum is usually coarsely milled into the semolina used to make the stiff doughs needed for dried pastas.

Consumers, and even commercial bakers, do not usually buy hard wheat flours or soft wheat flours per se. The various wheat flours available in the supermarket or specialty foods store are designated as all-purpose, self-rising, whole wheat, bread, graham, unbleached, or bromated. These descriptions are based on the grinding and blending operations at the miller's.

The first step in converting grain to flour is milling, a process designed to first separate the grain's endosperm (principally starch and protein) from its coating of bran and its germ. Wheat grains, like most cereals, are stored at less than 10% moisture to control spoilage, but must be conditioned to a slightly higher moisture content prior to milling. This toughens the bran and softens the endosperm, facilitating their separation. The wheat kernels are then passed between two grooved rollers turning at different speeds. This shearing action separates the endosperm from the bran and germ, which go on to further screening, grinding and separation. The liberated endosperm is further treated to remove any particles with bran remnants, and is then sent to the smooth surfaced reduction rolls. These rolls crush and grind to produce endosperm particles ranging from a coarse to fine particle size. The fine flour is sieved off and the coarser particles are sent to the next set of reduction rolls. This combination of reduction and sieving may be repeated several times.

Wheat endosperm is composed mostly, about 70% by weight, of starch grains, which are present in two basic sizes. The largest grains, about 0.0003 inch in diameter, constitute most of the weight of the starch in the endosperm. Milling results in three types of flour particles: those in the 0.0003 inch diameter range that are mostly starch, much smaller particles that are predominately protein plus small-grained starch, and larger chunks of protein with some associated starch. The white flours for baking contain all three particle types. A coarse, high protein fraction is also extracted from the milling process and sold as semolina, distinct from durum semolina but also intended for dried pastas.

Most baking flours are treated with a bleaching and aging agent. Flour in the U.S. is bleached with chlorine dioxide gas simply to obtain a uniform whiteness by oxidizing the small amount of natural yellow pigment. Bleaching also destroys the small amount of Vitamin E in the flour. The bleaching agent likewise ages the flour by modifying its proteins in such a way that desirable gluten formation is promoted. The chemical bleaching and aging practiced today is merely a practical alternative to the natural flour aging practiced for many years. White flours in the past would be stored for one or two months to allow oxygen from the air to have the same bleaching and gluten promoting effects that are derived from chlorine dioxide today. This natural oxidation was time and space consuming, and also somewhat undependable.

Unbleached flours, while obviously not bleached, are nonetheless aged, with potassium bromate or potassium iodate. Semolina is never bleached, primarily for reasons of tradition. Italian pastas have long been made from Mediterranean durum wheats with nearly double the yellow pigment content of most hard wheats. Pastas historically have therefore been yellow, and yellow they remain.

The last step before the final packaging of most white flour is addition of vitamin and mineral enrichment. About 95% of commercially produced white bread is enriched with added niacin, thiamin, riboflavin, iron, and in some cases calcium. Although not a federal regulation, many states mandate enrichment of white bread. The commercial bakers are free to add the enrichments themselves, but many prefer to use pre-enriched flour.

COMMON WHEAT FLOURS

A consumer's choice among the various wheat flours is based upon the miller's ability to combine the availability of both hard and soft wheats with his capability for producing flours with varying particle size and protein content.

ALL-PURPOSE FLOUR. This is a bleached, enriched blend of hard and soft wheat flours intended for use in a wide range of foods.

UNBLEACHED FLOUR. This is unbleached (but aged) all-purpose flour.

BREAD FLOUR. This is hard wheat flour which may or may not have added barley malt flour (food for the yeast) and potassium bromate (for gluten development).

BROMATED FLOUR. This is hard wheat flour to which up to 50 parts per million of potassium bromate has been added as a gluten developer. Bromated flours were developed primarily for biscuits but are used as well for bread. They promote a faster rising and more airy loaf.

HARD WHEAT FLOUR. This is simply what its name indicates, and is produced in both white and whole wheat. It is more likely found in a specialty food store than in a supermarket.

WHOLE WHEAT FLOUR. This is a medium-fine hard wheat flour with the germ retained but the bran either partially or totally removed.

GRAHAM FLOUR. This is supposed to be the entire coarsely ground wheat kernel (endosperm, germ, and bran). This name, however, is used loosely to include coarse whole wheat flours.

SELF-RISING FLOUR. This is soft wheat flour blended with sodium bicarbonate, monocalcium phosphate, and salt. It is popular for making biscuits, muffins and quick breads. Self-rising flour is sometimes sold as phosphated flour.

CAKE FLOUR. This is especially fine soft wheat flour that has been treated to weaken its gluten. This treatment allows incorporation of large amounts of shortening into mixtures and the development of good crumb in cakes and flakiness in pastries. Soft wheat flours are also used commercially for making doughnuts, cookies, crackers and pretzels.

GLUTEN FLOUR. This is white flour from which nearly all the starch has been removed. It is expensive and intended for dietetic purposes, but can be used in small amounts in breads made from grains like rye and barley that have little or no gluten.

OTHER FLOURS

While much less commonly available than wheat flours, meals or flours from other nutritional sources can be found, typically in health or specialty foods stores. They can be used in breads, and are useful as well for special culinary or nutritional purposes in most baking soda/acid leavened baked goods.

RYE FLOUR. This can vary from a light flour milled from endosperm to a very dark whole grain flour suitable for pumpernickel. Rye flour sold for bread baking may contain some hard wheat flour.

BARLEY FLOUR. This is generally a light, high protein, very low gluten flour milled from whole hulled barley.

TRITICALE FLOUR. This is a low gluten wheat-rye crossbreed produced for developing countries because of its high protein content. Although perishable and not widely available in this country, it is a good pastry flour and useful for high protein bread, although gentler kneading is required.

SOY FLOUR. In the strictest sense, this is flour milled from raw soybeans while soya flour is milled from toasted soybeans. Soy flour is generally milled from whole soybeans into one of three types of flour - full-fat, low-fat or defatted. Full-fat flour is the type usually available in stores for use in home baking. Because of its strong nutty flavor it is often used with other flours, or in recipes with spices, nuts or chocolate to mask its taste. Soy flour is used in baked goods for its high protein and ability to retard staling.

CORN FLOUR. This is the finest fraction obtained from the milling of corn endosperm. In descending order of size, the other fractions are segregated for cornflakes, grits, coarse corn meal and fine corn meal.

OAT FLOUR. This is the fine fraction resulting from the dehulling of the oat grain prior to the rolling of the oat groats. This flour contains no gluten, and is used in place of rolled oats (oatmeal) in baked goods. The addition of oat flour to home-baked products is used to maintain freshness longer, since oats contain a strong natural antioxidant.

RICE FLOUR. This is milled from broken kernels of white or brown rice and contains no gluten. Rice flour imparts a slightly grainy texture. Since it is essentially tasteless, it can be used in many types of baked goods, especially those with strongly flavored flours, like soy or rye.

Because nonwheat flours contain little or no gluten, they are most successfully used in baking soda/acid leavened rather than yeast leavened recipes. For those interested in exploring the nutritional or culinary possibilities of substituting the more common nonwheat flours in whole or part for wheat flour in recipes, the following table can be used as a guide.

Substitutes for 1 Cup of Wheat Flour in Baked Products

Rye Flour	1¼ cups
Oat Flour	1⅓ cups
Corn Flour	1 cup
Soy Flour	1½ cups
Barley Flour	1⅓ cups
Rice Flour	1 cup minus 2 tablespoons

Combinations of flours tend to produce better results. For example, a mixture of 1 cup minus 2 tablespoons of rice flour and 1¼ cups of rye flour will substitute for 2 cups of wheat flour. The bland flavor of the rice flour minimizes the strong rye taste, while the rye flour minimizes the grainy texture produced by the rice flour.

There are other less well known but highly nutritious flours that can be blended with wheat flour for distinctive results in soda/acid leavened baked goods.

AMARANTH FLOUR. Amaranth is an ancient South American low gluten grain which has been rediscovered by American consumers only within the past decade or so. It is higher in protein than corn or beans, higher in fiber than wheat, rice, soybeans or corn, the highest in iron of the cereal grains and rich in vitamins. It also contains the essential amino acid lysine, which is absent in most other cereal grains. The flour is milled from the whole grain. A blend of amaranth and whole wheat is reported to rival meat or eggs as a complete protein source.

QUINOA FLOUR. Quinoa (KEEN-wah) is another recent rediscovery of ancient South American origin. Like amaranth, it contains the essential amino acid lysine, and is high in protein and iron. Unlike amaranth, it is not a grain but the fruit of an herb. Quinoa flour is milled from the whole "grain" and is very low in gluten.

BUCKWHEAT FLOUR. Buckwheat is a cereal grass, not a grain, and resembles wheat in name only. It contains twice the B vitamins of wheat and is best known for its use in pancakes. The dark flour is milled from the unhulled groat, while the light flour is milled from the hulled groat and has a more delicate flavor.

MILLET FLOUR. This is ground from the whole hulled grain and contains no gluten. Millet is considered one of the most nutritious grains, and owing to its alkaline nature is sometimes recommended in diets for people with ulcers or colitis.

TEFF FLOUR. A newcomer to the U.S. via its ancient roots in Africa, Teff boasts higher iron than wheat, rice, millet or oats. The flour is milled from the whole grain, which can be either white, red, or brown. The white variety imparts the mildest flavor.

LEAVENING AGENTS

As explained previously, leavening is simply the act of introducing gas bubbles into a dough or batter so that it expands. The three basic approaches to leavening are generation of carbon dioxide by the reaction of baking soda with an acid, generation of carbon dioxide by fermentation of yeast, and mechanical incorporation of air by whipping or beating.

SODA/ACID. The baking soda/baking acid leavening system was detailed in Section 3. In short, the combination of baking soda with an acid liberates carbon dioxide that causes the batter or dough to expand. This is a rapid effect compared to yeast leavening, although there is some control over just how quickly the carbon dioxide is released depending on the particular acid used. For example, the fastest leavening action is with baking soda/cream of tartar; the single acting baking soda/monocalcium phosphate releases about two thirds of its carbon dioxide during mixing and the rest in response to oven heat; the double acting soda/monocalcium phosphate/sodium aluminum sulfate blend releases one third of its carbon dioxide during mixing and two thirds in the oven.

Baking soda is often used in recipes with naturally acid ingredients like sour milk, buttermilk, yogurt, molasses, chocolate and fruit preserves. The following combinations can serve as a guide to the use of baking soda with some common, naturally acidic ingredients; each is equivalent to two teaspoons of baking powder.

(A) ½ teaspoon baking soda per cup of buttermilk

(B) ½ teaspoon baking soda per cup of milk which has been soured with 1 tablespoon of white vinegar or lemon juice

(C) ½ teaspoon baking soda per cup of milk which has been soured with 1¾ teaspoons cream of tartar

(D) ½ teaspoon baking soda per cup of molasses

(E) ½ teaspoon baking soda per 1¼ teaspoons cream of tartar

YEAST. Yeast for baking is available in two forms. Yeast cake, or compressed yeast, is approximately 70% water versus less than 10% water in active dry yeast. Yeast cake is the more perishable of the two, but slightly more active in doughs. The two forms are produced from different strains of *Saccharomyces cerevisiae*, and both maintain their activity best when frozen. The principle source of yeast for baking is the brewing industry, although the "brewers yeast" sold in grocery and health food stores is not active and provides nutritional rather than leavening benefits.

Yeast feeds on sugars and produces primarily carbon dioxide and alcohol, although there are many other byproducts produced in minute quantity in a dough that together give the distinctively characteristic flavor of a yeast leavened product. The simple sugars like glucose and fructose are readily consumed and then after a slight time lag the yeast feeds on the maltose that malt enzymes produce from damaged starch granules in the flour. Adding limited amounts of sugar to a dough will increase yeast activity. Too much sugar will tend to dehydrate the yeast cells and reduce their activity. This is why sweet breads usually require extra yeast and why cookie and cake batters are generally inappropriate for yeast. Excess salt has the same inhibiting effect as sugar. The activity of hydrated yeast peaks at about 95°F, but 80°F is considered the optimum temperature for raising dough. Gas output is lower than at the warmer temperature, but so is the generation of sour byproducts.

Yeast fermentation produces small amounts of acids, so that as much as ¼ teaspoon of baking soda per cup of flour can be added to accelerate the rising of yeast leavened breads. This can be a little tricky since enough fermentation must occur to neutralize all the baking soda. An alternative approach is to grow active dry yeast in acidic fruit juice overnight. This can then be used in a dough or batter with the baking soda. Thin batters can be baked immediately. Thick batters or doughs can be left to raise in a warm spot for up to a half hour before baking.

Sourdoughs are a product of both yeast and bacterial fermentation. The yeasts are native airborne varieties that thrive in a more acidic environment than those derived from brewing. These yeasts cannot metabolize maltose at all, and serve as a perfect complement to the lactobacillus bacteria that thrive on it. These bacteria produce the acids - mostly lactic acid and some acetic acid - that account for sourdough's distinctive taste. The different strains of yeast and lactobacillus bacteria native to different parts of the U.S. lend a regional distinctness to sourdough breads produced in different parts of the country. The reason San Francisco sourdough is so prized and so essentially irreproducible elsewhere is that its bacteria is so unique to the bay area that it bears its own name, *lactobacillus sanfrancisco*. Likewise, a sourdough starter transplanted from San Francisco will eventually be changed by the bacteria indigenous to its new home.

AIR. Prior to soda/acid leavening, thin batters, as for pancakes and waffles, and raised cakes were aerated mechanically. In simplest form this involved tediously whipping air into the batter and then cooking before all the air could escape. Beaten eggs and especially well beaten egg whites can retain a fair amount of air bubbles and were often used. Creamed butter and sugar, whipped to a light texture was also a common way to incorporate air into a cake batter.

Mechanical leavening is still used in preparing batters today, but as a complement to soda/acid leavening. Vegetable shortenings have replaced butter because they can incorporate more air and form smaller air pockets. Electric mixers have replaced hand beating and whipping to produce the smallest and most uniformly distributed air pockets. The carbon dioxide liberated from the soda/acid reaction then expands the air pockets and completes the leavening.

OTHER INGREDIENTS

While flour and leavening form the foundation, the amount of water and a limited number of other ingredients determines the particular character of most baked goods, differentiating the breads from the biscuits, the rolls from the cakes, the crumbly from the flaky.

SHORTENING. The term "shortening" was coined in the early nineteenth century for oils or fats added to baked goods. These were supposed to "shorten" or break up the gluten to give the product a more tender crumb. The behavior of fats and oils in baking is actually more complicated, depending on the particular type and the amount used.

The liquid shortenings used today are vegetable oils. The home baker has the ready choice of corn, safflower, sunflower, olive and canola oil. Oils are used in relatively small amounts to add moistness and tenderness to cakes, waffles, pancakes, breads and in general any batter product that cooks to a crumb texture. The most widely used solid shortenings are based on hydrogenated vegetable oils. The hydrogenation process raises the melting point of the oil to above room temperature and produces the optimal fat crystal size to readily incorporate large amounts of air on subsequent whipping. Commercial solid shortenings like Crisco® are hydrogenated vegetable oil that has already been whipped to incorporate very fine air bubbbles. The alternative to this type of shortening is hand creamed butter or margarine.

Pastry calls for solid shortening so that alternate layers of dough and fat will produce the desired flakiness. Use of chilled utensils and surfaces is usually recommended for preparation of pastry doughs to avoid melting of the shortening and consequent loss of flakiness. Solid shortenings are used in cakes not to promote flakiness, but to provide a more moist and tender crumb. This can be achieved with oil alone, but the solid shortening provides leavening as well from the fine air bubbles it brings to the batter.

Shortening is also used in some bread doughs, but for a function contrary to its name. Small amounts of oil or fat do add to moistness and tenderness, as in cakes, but they also promote greater loaf volume. One theory holds that this is due to a lubricating effect whereby the shortening actually allows for added lengthening of the gluten, making it more extensible and resulting in a bigger loaf.

EGGS. Eggs are used in batters mainly for their protein and fat contributions. On heating, egg protein coagulates into films or filaments that help retain the leavening gases and form an open cell or crumb structure. The egg fats serve the same function as added shortening. Beaten egg whites will hold large amounts of air and are often used with creamed butter or margarine or commercial shortening to leaven cakes.

MILK. Milk provides water and, like eggs, protein and fat that contribute to crumb structure and tenderness. Milk also accelerates surface browning. Milk must be scalded and cooled prior to use in yeast leavened products to alter milk serum proteins which would otherwise interact with flour proteins and produce a slack and sticky dough.

SUGAR. Sugar (and its functional, nutritional and caloric equivalents, honey, molasses, corn syrup, brown sugar and malt syrup) is used principally as a sweetener in batters and doughs, and a promoter of surface browning. In moderate amounts, sugar is a nutrient for yeast, while at high levels it inhibits fermentation. Sugar is also hygroscopic (attracts water) and retards gluten development by competing with the flour for available water. That is why yeast raised sweet doughs take longer to develop, while after baking they give moist and tender products that stay fresh longer. The sugar holds on to water and retards staling. The enhanced browning caused by sugar can also provide, as a side effect, a more moist product, since it prompts removal from the oven sooner.

SALT. Like sugar, salt is used in batters and doughs principally for taste. In bread doughs, excess salt inhibits yeast activity and stiffens gluten, markedly reducing its extensibility. Compact, dense loaves result. At normal use levels, salt still inhibits somewhat the elasticity of gluten, but prevents it from being weakened into a sticky mass by also inhibiting the activity of protein digesting enzymes in the flour.

THE BAKING PROCESS

For aerated products like breads, biscuits, quick breads, rolls, muffins, pancakes, scones and waffles, the baking process balances the formation and growth of entrapped gas bubbles with the gelatinization of the flour's starch and transition of the elastic protein structure from stretched to set.

In yeast leavened doughs, the open cell structure is largely established by the raising process before baking. When placed in the oven, the dough goes through a rapid additional expansion (oven spring) because of the growth of gas cells from a combination of steam, accelerated metabolism of the yeast, and the physical expansion of gas at elevated temperatures. The heat, however, soon kills the yeast (halting fermentation), causes the starch to gel, and sets the gluten structure. In a conventional oven, this process proceeds from the outside of the loaf inward so that ultimate loaf size is established during the early stages of baking. As heat penetrates the loaf's interior to complete this process, surface browning occurs. Ideally, a golden brown outside will signal a fully cooked inside. Fully cooked, of course, is largely a matter of taste once the center of the loaf is no longer dough. After the structure (the crumb) at the center of the loaf is set, further cooking lowers the moisture content of the bread while further browning the crust. This browning is not strictly a cosmetic phenomenon, however. The browning reactions produce much of the flavor that works its way into the loaf.

In soda/acid leavened doughs like quick breads and biscuits, or batters like pancakes and cookies, little or no cell structure is established before baking. A fast acting system, like baking soda with cream of tartar, necessitates quick, coarse blending of ingredients just prior to placing in a hot oven. Most of the gas cells are established prior to exposure to heat. Heat and generated steam cause them to expand; a thick batter or dough will be more successful in keeping these gas cells contained. The size and quantity of ultimately retained cells will depend on the nature of the protein structure formed by the combination of flour, egg and milk proteins, and how quickly this structure will set. Thin batters, as for pancakes, require high heat and relatively short cooking times to balance gas evolution with the setting of the protein structure so that a light airy texture is obtained. Thicker batters, as for quick breads and muffins, will retain the liberated leavening gases longer, allowing for the surface crust to develop and further control loss, while enabling the more gradual cooking of the product's interior.

A slower acting system, like the double acting baking powders, allows for more leeway in the time between mixing and baking since it is the heat of the oven that catalyzes the soda-acid reaction. In this case, slower baking, or a lower oven temperature, is usually preferred so that the starch does not gel and the protein structure does not set well before the gas evolution is complete. This is also what makes possible "cold oven" baking, placing a dough or batter in a cold oven and then turning up the heat. The heating of the oven to baking temperature gives the leavening process a head start.

For most baked goods, staling is not simply the loss of moisture it appears to be. During baking, water is released from the flour proteins and absorbed by the starch. The originally semicrystalline starch becomes an amorphous gel. The process is essentially the same as using flour to thicken a sauce. Before the gelatinization temperature of the starch (at about 140°F), the sauce remains thin. At this temperature, the sauce suddenly thickens as the starch absorbs water and forms a gel. Likewise, a bread, cake or cookie fresh from the oven has a soft consistency because the starch is still gelled. On cooling, most of the starch looses water and reverts from gelatinous to semicrystalline. Most of this water is lost through the crust or outer surfaces as steam. This is the reason why freshly baked bread, for instance, should not be kept in its pan long enough to become totally cooled. The trapped steam will make the crust soggy.

A small fraction of starch remains gelatinized even after cooling and only slowly releases water, which migrates to the outer surfaces. These surfaces, which are drier than the interior due to desiccation in the oven, will absorb this water in their dehydrated starch and protein. A bread crust, for example, will turn from dry and crisp to tough and leathery; a cookie or cracker will turn from crisp to soft. Left uncovered, the baked good will eventually loose all of its moisture and become irreversibly dried out. Well wrapped goods will also stale, but reversibly. Wrapping tightly and reheating to the gelatinization temperature of the starch will cause reabsorption of available water and re-"freshing." This works well for breads, although a crisp crust will never be regained. This water transport mechanism also explains how the water holding nature of sugar and other sweeteners keep sweet goods fresher longer than unsweetened products.

It is a peculiarity of the starch in flour that, in the process of cooling the starch gel (such as exists in freshly baked goods) to room temperature (recrystallization) and then to freezing, its water holding capacity is at a minimum just prior to the freezing point. That is why, contrary to intuition, freshly baked bread will actually stale more quickly when stored wrapped in the refrigerator than when kept well wrapped at room temperature. This is also why it is best to freeze homemade breads, rolls, muffins, etc. that will not be served within a few days. Commercially baked goods and homebaked goods from prepared mixes usually last considerably longer under refrigeration, or at room temperature for that matter, because most contain emulsifiers to control the movement and loss of moisture over time.

The following section combines the above ingredients, plus some delicious additions, to provide a sampling of recipes demonstrating the use of baking soda to full advantage. Most of these recipes employ all-purpose flour, but the adventurous are encouraged to experiment with flour blends to develop your own unique adaptations. As you bake and sample each creation, you can reflect on the physical and chemical processes which conspired to such pleasing ends, or, better yet, just enjoy.

QUICK BREADS & MUFFINS

All of the quick breads which follow are meant to be baked in a 9x5x2½ inch loaf pan unless otherwise indicated. The muffins can be baked in either 2½ inch or 4 inch muffin cups as you prefer. The size indicated is the size we preferred. Cultured buttermilk powder is used (we use SACO's) instead of fresh buttermilk not just for convenience. You can vary the intensity of buttermilk flavor desired, or adjust for the amount of baking soda used by adding more or less buttermilk powder without changing the amount of liquid.

DATE-NUT BREAD

2½ cups all-purpose flour
1¼ teaspoons baking soda
½ cup brown sugar
1 teaspoon salt
1 cup chopped dates
¾ cup chopped walnuts
2 eggs, beaten
¾ cup milk
5 tablespoons white vinegar
¼ cup vegetable shortening, melted

Preheat oven to 350°. Blend the dry ingredients and then stir in the dates and walnuts. Blend the milk, vinegar and melted shortening into the beaten eggs. Stir the liquid into the dry ingredients; mix only until smooth. Bake for about 60 minutes or until a cake tester inserted in center comes out clean. Cool in pan for 10 minutes and then on rack to room temperature.

OLD-FASHIONED CORN BREAD

1 cup all-purpose flour
1½ cup yellow cornmeal
½ cup cultured buttermilk powder
¾ teaspoon baking soda
1 teaspoon salt
2 eggs, beaten
1½ cups water
3 tablespoons vegetable shortening, melted

Preheat oven to 425°. Blend the dry ingredients. With an electric mixer, beat the eggs, water and melted shortening. Add the liquid ingredients to the dry, stirring only until smooth. Turn into a well-greased 8" x 8" pan. Bake for about 25 minutes or until a cake tester inserted in center comes out clean. Serve hot.

PUMPKIN BREAD

3 cups all-purpose flour
1 cup sugar
2 teaspoons baking soda
2 teaspoons cinnamon
1 teaspoon nutmeg
½ teaspoon salt
¼ teaspoon cream of tartar
1 cup raisins
1 cup roasted cashews, chopped
3 eggs, beaten
1½ cups canned pumpkin filling
¼ cup corn oil
1 cup water

Preheat oven to 350°. Blend the dry ingredients and then blend in the raisins and cashews. With an electric mixer, beat the eggs, pumpkin and oil. Add the water and whip briefly. Stir the liquid into the dry blend and mix only until smooth. Bake for about 75 minutes or until a cake tester inserted in the center comes out clean. Cool in pan for 10 minutes and then on rack to room temperature.

BUTTERMILK AMARANTH/CORN BREAD

2½ cups all-purpose flour
1½ cups amaranth flour or yellow corn meal
¾ cup cultured buttermilk powder
⅓ cup sugar
2 teaspoons baking soda
2 eggs, beaten
½ cup corn oil
2 cups water

Preheat oven to 350°. Blend dry ingredients. Add oil and water to beaten eggs. Stir liquid into dry ingredients and mix only until smooth. Bake for about 60 minutes or until a cake tester inserted in center comes out clean. Cool in pan for 10 minutes and then on rack to room temperature.

HARVEST BREAD

2½ cups all-purpose flour
½ cup yellow corn meal
½ cup quick cooking oats
1 cup brown sugar
2 teaspoons baking soda
2 teaspoons cinnamon
1 cup raisins
2 eggs, beaten
½ cup canned pumpkin filling
½ cup tomato ketchup

¼ cup corn oil
1½ cups apple juice

Preheat oven to 350°. Blend the dry ingredients and then stir in the raisins. With an electric mixer, beat the eggs, pumpkin, ketchup and oil. Add the apple juice and whip briefly. Stir the liquid into the dry blend and mix only until smooth. Bake for about 75 minutes or until a cake tester inserted in the center comes out clean. Cool in pan for 10 minutes and then on rack to room temperature.

EGGPLANT/ZUCCHINI BREAD

2 cups all-purpose flour
1½ cups sugar
2¼ teaspoons baking soda
3 teaspoons cinnamon
1 teaspoon nutmeg
¼ teaspoon cream of tartar
1 cup raisins
2 cups peeled eggplant (not too wet or seedy) or zucchini,
  coarsely grated
3 eggs, beaten
1 cup corn oil
2 teaspoons vanilla

Preheat oven to 375°. Blend the dry ingredients and then stir in the raisins and eggplant or zucchini. Add the oil and vanilla to the beaten eggs. Add the liquid to the dry blend, stirring only until smooth. Bake for about 70 minutes or until a cake tester inserted in center comes out clean. Cool in pan for 10 minutes and then on rack to room temperature.

NOUVELLE CORN BREAD

2½ cups all-purpose flour
1 cup yellow corn meal
2 teaspoons baking soda
1 teaspoon salt
¾ cup shredded whole milk mozarella cheese
2 eggs, beaten
1½ cups milk
⅓ cup balsamic vinegar
⅓ cup olive oil

Preheat oven to 350°. Blend the dry ingredients and then stir in the mozarella. With stirring, add the milk, vinegar and oil in order to the beaten eggs. Add the liquid to the dry blend, stirring only until smooth. Bake for about 45 minutes or until a cake tester inserted in center comes out clean. Cool in pan for 10 minutes and then on rack to room temperature.

SIMPLE SODA BREAD

4 cups sifted all-purpose flour
½ cup cultured buttermilk powder
1 tablespoon sugar
2 teaspoons baking soda
1 teaspoon salt
1 cup raisins
1½ cups cold water
⅓ cup olive oil

Preheat oven to 350°. Blend the dry ingredients and then stir in raisins. Add water and stir to a soft dough. Knead in oil. Turn onto lightly floured surface and knead to form a smooth ball. Pat by hand on greased baking sheet to about 1½ inch thickness. With sharp knife score into 4 sections. Bake 45 minutes or until bread is browned and a cake tester inserted in the center comes out clean. Best served warm with butter.

ZUCCHINI MUFFINS

2 cups all-purpose flour
¾ cup sugar
¾ teaspoon baking soda
¾ teaspoon baking powder
¾ teaspoon salt
1 teaspoon cinnamon
1 teaspoon nutmeg
1 cup zucchini, coarsely grated
½ cup raisins
½ cup chopped walnuts
3 eggs, beaten
¾ cup corn oil
2 teaspoons vanilla

Preheat oven to 375°. Blend the dry ingredients and then stir in the zucchini, raisins and walnuts. Blend the oil and vanilla into the beaten eggs. Stir the liquid into the dry ingredients and mix only until smooth. Fill 6 lightly greased 4 inch muffin cups about ⅔ full. Bake for about 25 minutes or until a cake tester inserted in center comes out clean. Serve warm, or cool in cups for 10 minutes and then on rack to room temperature.

APPLE NUT MUFFINS

1½ cups all-purpose flour
½ cup quick cooking oats
⅔ cup brown sugar
1 teaspoon baking soda
2 teaspoons cream of tartar
1 teaspoon cinnamon

½ teaspoon salt
¼ teaspoon ground nutmeg
1 cup coarsely chopped peeled apple
½ cup chopped walnuts
½ cup raisins
2 eggs, beaten
¼ cup cold milk
½ cup stick margarine, just melted

Preheat oven to 400°. Blend the dry ingredients and then mix in the apples, walnuts and raisins. Blend the milk and melted margarine into the beaten eggs. Stir the liquid mixture into the dry ingredients and mix only until moistened. Fill 6 lightly greased 4 inch muffin cups. Bake for about 15 minutes or until a cake tester inserted in center comes out clean. Serve warm, or cool in cups for 10 minutes and then on rack to room temperature.

BROWN BREAD MUFFINS

2 cups whole wheat flour
⅔ cup all-purpose flour
⅔ cup brown sugar
2 teaspoons baking soda
⅔ cup cultured buttermilk powder
1 teaspoon nutmeg
¾ cup raisins
2 cups water

Preheat oven to 350°. Blend the dry ingredients and then stir in the raisins. Stir the water into the dry ingredients and mix only until smooth. Fill 6 lightly greased 4 inch muffin cups about ⅔ full. Bake for about 35 minutes or until a cake tester inserted in center comes out clean. Serve warm, or cool in cups for 10 minutes and then on rack to room temperature.

BANANA OAT RAISIN MUFFFINS

1½ cups quick cooking oats
½ cup all-purpose flour
½ cup whole wheat flour
1 teaspoon baking soda
1 teaspoon baking powder
½ teaspoon salt
1 cup raisins
1 egg, beaten
1 cup milk
1 cup pureed ripe banana
¼ cup corn oil
2 teaspoons vanilla

Preheat oven to 400°. Blend the dry ingredients and then mix in the raisins. Blend the milk, banana, oil and vanilla into the beaten eggs. Stir the liquid mixture into the dry ingredients and mix only until moistened. Fill 12 lightly greased 2½ inch muffin cups. Bake for about 20 minutes or until a cake tester inserted in center comes out clean. Serve warm, or cool in cups for 10 minutes and then on rack to room temperature.

COOKIES

BIG & EASY OATMEAL COOKIES

3 cups quick cooking oats
1 cup all-purpose flour
1½ cups brown sugar
1 teaspoon baking soda
1 cup raisins
1 cold egg, beaten
¼ cup cold water

2 teaspoons vanilla
¾ cup stick margarine, just melted

Preheat oven to 350°. Blend the dry ingredients and then stir in the raisins. Blend the cold water, vanilla and melted margarine into the beaten egg. Stir the liquid into the dry mixture only until evenly moistened. Shape with floured hands into 1½ inch balls and place 2 inches apart on lightly greased cookie sheets. Bake for 18-20 minutes or until lightly browned. Cool on cookie sheets for 3 minutes and then on rack to room temperature. Makes 1½ - 2 dozen cookies.

BIRTHDAY COOKIE

1½ cups all-purpose flour
¾ cup brown sugar
1 teaspoon baking soda
½ teaspoon salt
1½ cups semisweet chocolate morsels
1 cold egg, beaten
¼ cup corn syrup
2 teaspoons vanilla
½ cup stick margarine, just melted

Blend the dry ingredients; stir in the morsels. Blend the syrup, vanilla and melted margarine into the beaten egg. Stir the liquid into the dry mixture only until evenly moistened. Refrigerate covered for at least one hour. Preheat oven to 325°. Grease a round 12 inch foil baking pan; spread dough to within 1½ inches of edge. Spell out birthday greeting with additional morsels lightly pressed in surface. Place pan on cookie sheet and bake for about 30 minutes or until edges are firm. Place foil pan on rack and cool to room temperature.

TOLL HOUSE® REDUX

3¾ cups all-purpose flour
2 cups brown sugar
2½ teaspoons baking soda
¾ teaspoon salt
2 cups semisweet chocolate morsels
1½ cups mayonnaise (the real stuff)
¾ cup stick margarine, just melted

Preheat oven to 350°. Blend the dry ingredients and then stir in the morsels. With an electric mixer, whip the melted margarine into the mayonnaise and then add to dry mixture. Beat briefly to a coarse dough. Shape into 1½ inch balls and place 2 inches apart on lightly greased cookie sheets. Bake for about 15 minutes or until lightly browned. Cool on cookie sheets for 3 minutes and then on rack to room temperature. Makes 3 - 4 dozen cookies.

ORANGE APRICOT COOKIES

1 cup all-purpose flour
¾ cup whole wheat flour
¼ cup sugar
½ teaspoon baking soda
½ teaspoon cinnamon
¼ teaspoon salt
¾ cup dried apricots, chopped
1 teaspoon grated orange rind
½ cup fresh orange juice
¼ cup corn oil
1 egg, beaten

Preheat oven to 375°. Blend the dry ingredients and then stir in the chopped apricots and orange rind. Blend the orange juice, oil and egg. Add the liquid mixture to the dry ingredients and mix until uniform. Drop by tablespoonfuls about 1 inch apart onto ungreased cookie sheets. Bake for about 10 minutes or until lightly browned. Cool on cookie sheets for 3 minutes and then on rack to room temperature. Makes 3 - 4 dozen cookies.

PEANUT BUTTER CHOCOLATE COOKIES

¾ cup sugar
⅔ cup stick margarine, softened
2 eggs, beaten
1 teaspoon vanilla
6 oz. semisweet chocolate, melted
1½ cups all-purpose flour
2 cups quick cooking oats
1 teaspoon baking soda
2 cups peanut butter chips

With an electric mixer, cream the sugar and margarine. Add the eggs and vanilla and beat until smooth. Add the melted chocolate and beat until smooth. Blend the oats, flour and baking soda. Gradually beat this dry blend into the liquid mixture. Mix only until uniformly moistened. Mix in the peanut butter chips. Refrigerate covered for at least one hour. Preheat oven to 350°. Shape dough into 1½ inch balls and place 2 inches apart on lightly greased cookie sheets. Bake for about 15 minutes or until lightly browned. Cool on cookie sheets for 3 minutes and then on rack to room temperature. Makes 3 - 4 dozen cookies.

CHOCOLATE PEANUT BUTTER COOKIES

1½ cups brown sugar
1 cup stick margarine, softened
2 cups chunky peanut butter

2 eggs, beaten
2 teaspoons butter extract
2 cups all-purpose flour
2 teaspoons baking soda
¼ teaspoon salt
2 cups semisweet chocolate morsels

With an electric mixer, cream the sugar, margarine and peanut butter. Add the eggs and extract and beat until smooth. Blend the flour, baking soda and salt. Gradually beat this dry blend into the liquid mixture. Mix only until uniformly moistened. Mix in the morsels. Refrigerate covered for at least one hour. Preheat oven to 375°. Shape dough into 1½ inch balls and place 2 inches apart on lightly greased cookie sheets. Bake for about 15 minutes or until lightly browned. Cool on cookie sheets for 3 minutes and then on rack to room temperature. Makes 2 - 3 dozen cookies.

BRAN APPLE BARS

1 cup whole-bran cereal
½ cup skim milk
1 cup all-purpose flour
½ teaspoon baking soda
½ teaspoon cinnamon
¼ teaspoon nutmeg
⅓ cup stick margarine, softened
½ cup brown sugar
2 egg whites
1 cup pared and chopped apple

Preheat oven to 350°. Soak bran in milk until milk is absorbed. Blend dry ingredients. In a separate bowl, cream the margarine and sugar with an electric mixer. Add the egg whites and beat well. Add the dry ingredients and mix until just smooth. Stir in the bran mixture and apples. Pour into lightly greased 9 x 9 inch baking pan. Bake 30 minutes or until cake tester inserted in center comes out clean. Cool on rack to room temperature.

BREAKFAST

ORANGE RAISIN SCONES

3 cups all-purpose flour
½ cup sugar
2 teaspoons baking soda
½ cup cold stick margarine, sliced
1 cup raisins
1 cold egg, beaten
½ cup orange juice

Preheat oven to 350°. Blend the flour, sugar and baking soda. With an electric mixer, cut in the margarine until the mixture resembles coarse meal. Stir in the raisins. Blend the orange juice into the egg. Add the liquid mixture to the dry ingredients and mix until uniform. Gather dough into ball. Roll dough to ½ inch thickness on lightly floured surface. Cut into 3 inch circles. Place on lightly greased baking sheets about ½ inch apart. Bake for about 15 minutes or until slightly browned.

GRAHAM BUTTERMILK PANCAKES

2 cups all-purpose flour
½ cup crushed graham crackers (3 whole crackers)
½ cup cultured buttermilk powder
2 tablespoons sugar
2 teaspoons baking soda
½ teaspoon salt
2 eggs, beaten
4 tablespoons corn oil

2 teaspoons vanilla
2 cups water

Blend the dry ingredients. Add the oil, vanilla and water to the beaten eggs. Stir liquid into dry ingredients only until smooth. Pour batter onto a hot, lightly greased griddle. Cook until bubbles rise to the top and underside is lightly browned. Flip and brown on other side.

CORNMEAL PANCAKES

1 cup all-purpose flour
1 cup yellow cornmeal
⅓ cup instant nonfat milk powder
2 tablespoons sugar
2½ teaspoons baking soda
½ teaspoon cream of tartar
½ teaspoon salt
3 eggs, beaten
1 cup water
3 tablespoons stick margarine, melted

Blend the dry ingredients. Add the water and melted margarine to the beaten eggs. Stir liquid into dry ingredients only until smooth. Pour batter onto a hot, lightly greased griddle. Cook until bubbles rise to the top and underside is lightly browned. Flip and brown on other side.

WAFFLES

2 cups all-purpose flour
½ teaspoon baking soda
½ teaspoon salt
4 eggs
¼ cup sugar
2 cups plain yogurt or sour cream

Preheat waffle iron. Blend flour, baking soda and salt. In a separate bowl, beat eggs and sugar with electric mixer until thickened. Fold in dry mixture and yogurt or sour cream alternately, beginning and ending with dry mixture. Blend just until uniform.

ENGLISH MUFFIN LOAVES

6 cups all-purpose flour
2 pkgs. active dry yeast, quick rise
1 tablespoon sugar
2 teaspoons salt
¼ teaspoon baking soda
2½ cups low fat milk
cornmeal

Blend 3 cups flour, yeast, sugar, salt and baking soda. Heat the milk until very warm (120°-130°); do not boil. Add to dry mixture; beat well. Stir in remaining flour to make a stiff batter. Spoon into two 8½ x 4½ inch pans that have been greased and sprinkled with cornmeal. Cover; let rise in warm area for 45 minutes. Bake at 400° for 25 minutes. Remove from pans immediately and cool on rack to room temperature.

FUNNEL CAKES

1¼ cups all-purpose flour
2 tablespoons sugar
1 teaspoon baking soda
¾ teaspoon baking powder
¼ teaspoon salt
1 egg, beaten
¾ cup milk
powdered sugar
oil for frying

Heat ¼ inch of oil in a skillet. Blend dry ingredients. Blend beaten egg and milk, mix into dry ingredients and beat just until smooth. Using a funnel with at least ⅜ inch opening, cover bottom with finger and add ¼ cup of batter at a time. Holding the funnel over the center of the skillet, remove finger and release the batter into the hot oil in a slow spiral pattern. Fry 2 minutes or until golden brown, turning once. Drain on paper towels, sprinkle with powdered sugar. Serve hot with syrup.

DESSERTS

CRANBERRY CAKE

2¼ cups all-purpose flour
1½ cups quick cooking oats
1 tablespoon baking powder
½ teaspoon baking soda
2 cups chopped cranberries
¾ cup stick margarine, softened
1 cup sugar
1 cup milk
3 eggs
2 teaspoons orange extract

Preheat oven to 350°. Blend the dry ingredients and then stir in the cranberries. In a separate bowl, cream the margarine and sugar with an electric mixer until light and fluffy. Add the milk and then the eggs one at a time, beating after each addition. Stir in the extract. Add dry ingredients and beat until uniform. Turn into greased and floured 10 inch tube pan. Bake about 60 minutes or until cake tester inserted in center comes out clean. Cool in pan for 10 minutes and then on rack to room temperature. Drizzle with Yogurt Glaze when completely cooled.

YOGURT GLAZE

1½ cups plain nonfat yogurt
3 tablespoons brown sugar
2 teaspoons vanilla extract

Blend well until smooth.

BANANA CHIP CAKE

1¼ cups sifted cake flour
¾ teaspoon baking soda
½ teaspoon salt
½ cup vegetable shortening
1 cup sugar
2 eggs
¾ cup mashed banana (about 2 medium bananas)
1 cup chocolate minimorsels

Preheat oven to 350°. Blend the flour, baking soda and salt. Using an electric mixer, cream the shortening; gradually add sugar and continue beating until light and fluffy. Add eggs one at a time, beating after each addition. Blend in mashed banana. Add dry ingredients and minimorsels to banana mixture and mix well. Turn into greased and floured 9 inch square pan. Bake 35 minutes or until cake tester inserted in center comes out clean. Cool on rack to room temperature.

SOUR CREAM POUND CAKE

3 cups all-purpose flour
½ teaspoon baking soda
¼ teaspoon salt
3 cups sugar
1 cup stick margarine

6 eggs
1 cup sour cream
2 teaspoons vanilla

Preheat oven to 350°. Blend the flour, baking soda and salt. Using an electric mixer, cream the margarine and sugar until light and fluffy. Add eggs one at a time, beating after each addition. Stir in the sour cream and vanilla. Add dry ingredients and mix well. Turn into greased and floured 10 inch tube pan. Bake 85 minutes or until cake tester inserted in center comes out clean. Cool in pan for 10 minutes and then on rack to room temperature.

REALLY CHOCOLATE CAKE

2 cups cake flour
1 teaspoon baking soda
¾ teaspoon salt
½ cup vegetable shortening
1½ cups brown sugar
2 eggs
3 oz. unsweetened chocolate, melted
1 teaspoon vanilla
1 cup plus 2 tablespoons milk

Preheat oven to 350°. Blend the dry ingredients. In a separate bowl, cream the shortening and sugar with an electric mixer. Beat in eggs until very light and fluffy. Stir in the melted chocolate and vanilla. Beat in the dry mixture alternately with the milk, beginning and ending with dry ingredients. Beat after each addition until smooth and uniform. Pour into two greased and floured 9 inch layer pans. Bake 25 minutes or until cake tester inserted in center comes out clean. Cool in pans for 10 minutes and then on racks to room temperature. Frost with Fudge Frosting .

FUDGE FROSTING

1 cup granulated sugar
4 tablespoons unsweetened cocoa
4 tablespoons stick margarine
½ cup milk
2 tablespoons corn syrup
1 teaspoon vanilla extract
1 cup confectioners' sugar

Mix granulated sugar and cocoa in heavy saucepan. Add butter, milk and syrup; heat to boiling, stirring occasionally. Cool slightly. Beat in vanilla and confectioners' sugar; continue beating until thick enough to spread.

REALLY REALLY CHOCOLATE CAKE

2¾ cups cake flour
1 teaspoon baking soda
¼ teaspon salt
¾ cup stick margarine
6 oz. semisweet chocolate
1½ cups sugar
3 eggs
2 teaspoons vanilla
1½ cups water

Preheat oven to 350°. Blend the dry ingredients. Carefully melt the margarine and chocolate together with stirring just until the chocolate is completely melted. Blend in the sugar. With an electric mixer, beat in the eggs individually until smooth. Add the vanilla. Stir in ½ cup of the dry mixture. Beat in the remaining dry mixture alternately with the water until smooth and uniform. Pour into two greased and floured 9 inch layer pans. Bake 35 minutes or until cake tester inserted in center comes out clean. Cool in pans for 10 minutes and then on racks to room temperature. Frost with Fudge Frosting.

ALMOND POUND CAKE

2 cups all-purpose flour
¼ teaspoon baking soda
1½ teaspoons cream of tartar
1 cup sugar
7 oz. almond paste
1 cup stick margarine
4 eggs
½ cup milk

Preheat oven to 350°. Blend the first three ingredients. Cream the sugar, almond paste and margarine with an electric mixer. Beat in eggs individually until light and fluffy. Beat in the dry mixture alternately with the milk, beginning and ending with dry mix. Beat until uniform. Pour into greased, floured Bundt pan. Bake 70 minutes or until cake tester inserted in center comes out clean. Cool in pan for 10 minutes and then on rack to room temperature. Drizzle with Chocolate Glaze if desired.

CHOCOLATE GLAZE

⅓ cup stick margarine
2 cups confectioner's sugar
2 teaspoons vanilla
2 oz. unsweetened chocolate, melted
2 tablespoons hot water

Melt the margarine in a sauce pan over medium heat. Stir in the sugar, vanilla, chocolate and water until well blended. If too thick, blend in additional hot water one tablespoon at a time until glaze is desired consistency.

BIBLIOGRAPHY

**American Chemical Industry:
A History**
William Haynes
Van Nostrand New York 1949

American Food
Evan Jones
Dutton New York 1975

**Appleton's Cyclopaedia of
American Biography**
James Grant Wilson
& John Fiske
Appleton New York 1887

**The Babbitt Family History
1643-1900**
William Bradford Browne
C. Hack & Son
Taunton, MA 1912

**A Bibliography for Culinary
Historians Using the Harvard
University Libraries and the
Arthur and Elizabeth Schlesinger
Library of the History of Women
in America**
Barbara Ketcham Wheaton
& Patricia M. Kelly
Cambridge 1985

The Book of Bread
Judith & Evan Jones
Harper & Row
New York 1982

**Carla Emery's Old Fashioned
Recipe Book**
Carla Emery
Bantam New York 1977

The Chemistry of the Arts
Arthur L. Porter
Carey & Lea
Philadelphia 1830

The Complete Food Handbook
Roger P. Doyle
& James L. Redding
Grove Press New York 1976

**A Comprehensive Treaty on
Inorganic and Theoretical
Chemistry**
J.W. Mellor
Longmans London 1927

**Concise Dictionary of American
Biography, 2nd Ed.**
Scribner's New York 1977

The Cook's Companion
Dorris McFerran Townsend
Crown New York 1978

**Dictionary of American
Biography**
Allen Johnson
Scribner's New York 1928

**The Dictionary of Medical
Folklore**
Carol Ann Rinzler
Thomas Y. Crowell
New York 1979

Dictionary of National Biography
Leslie Stephen & Sidney Lee
Oxford University Press
Oxford 1917

Dictionary of Scientific Biography
Scribner's New York 1972

Eating In America
Waverly Root
& Richard de Rochemont
William Morrow
New York 1976

Eighty Years of Baking Powder History
Rumford Chemical Works
Rumford, RI 1939

Encyclopedia of Chemical Technology
Kirk-Othmer
Wiley New York 1st Ed., 1948
2nd Ed., 1964, 1978 3rd Ed.,1984

English Bread & Yeast Cookery
Elizabeth David
Viking   New York 1980

The Food Book
James Trager
Grossman New York 1970

Food in History
Reay Tannahill
Stein & Day New York 1973

Foods & Nutrition Encyclopedia
Pegus Press Clovis, CA 1983

Geology and World Deposits
Peter W. Harben
& Robert L. Bates
Metal Bulletin Plc London 1990

The Goldbeck's Guide To Good Food
Nikki & David Goldbeck
New American Library
New York 1987

The Grains Cookbook
Bert Greene
Workman Publishing
New York 1988

Great American Food Almanac
Irena Chalmers
& Milton Glaser
Harper & Row New York 1986

The Great American Medicine Show
David Armstrong
& Elizabeth Metzger Armstrong
Prentice Hall New York 1991

Great Oldtime Recipes
Beatriz-Maria Prada
Ballantine New York 1974

A History of American Manufacturers from 1608 to 1860
J. Leander Bishop
Edward Young London 1868

History of the City of New York 1609-1909
John William Leonard
Journal of Commerce and
Commercial Bulletin
New York 1910

Hung, Strung & Potted
Sally Smith Booth
Clarkson N. Potter
New York 1971

The Ingenious Yankees
Joseph & Frances Geis
Thomas Y. Crowell
New York 1976

Inventors Who Left Their Brands On America
Frank H. Olsen
Bantam New York 1991

Kitchen Science
Howard Hillman
Houghton Mifflin Boston 1989

Listening To America
Stuart Berg Flexner
Simon and Schuster
New York 1982

Made In USA
Phil Patton
Grove Weidenfield
New York 1992

The National Cyclopaedia of American Biography
University Microfilms 1967

New and Improved: The Story of Mass Marketing in America
Richard S. Tedlow
Basic Books New York 1990

On Food And Cooking
Harold McGee
Scribner's New York 1984

Panati's Extraordinary Origins of Everyday Things
Charles Panati
Harper & Row New York 1987

Revolution At The Table
Harvey H. Levenstein
Oxford University Press
New York 1988

The Rise and Decline of the Great Atlantic & Pacific Tea Company
William I. Walsh
Lyle Stuart
Secaucus, New Jersey 1986

Satisfaction Guaranteed: The Making of the American Mass Market
Susan Strasser
Pantheon New York 1989

The Secret Life of Food
Martin Elkort
Jeremy P. Tarcher
Los Angeles 1991

Sodium Bicarbonate
Church & Dwight
Princeton 1989

The Supermarket Handbook
Nikki & David Goldbeck
New American Library
New York 1976

Saleratus

**The Versatile Grain and the
Elegant Bean**
Sheryl & Mel London
Simon & Schuster
New York 1992

Who Was Who In America
Marquis   Chicago   1963

INDEX

brewers 10
bromated flour 137
Bronson Alcott 25
buckwheat flour 141
buffer 56
Burgin & Sons 18

cadmium 123
cake flour 138
cake mixes 100
calomel 14
Canada 44, 51
canning, automatic 31
carbon dioxide 97
carbonate
  lead 112
  potassium 4
  sodium 6, 11
carbonation
  dry 7, 9, 16, 49
  solution 7
cardboard cartons 31
carpeting 125
cattle, beef 106
cavities 102
CEM Message 113
Central Pacific Railroad 29
Central Plains 29, 30
cerussite 112
chain store brands 39
chain stores 42
Charles Dickens, Mrs. 22
Charles Saunders 39
Charles Stillwell 31
chemical strippers 123
Chicago World's Fair 29
chicken feeds 106
chlorinated hydrocarbons 121, 122
chlorine dioxide 136
chlorofluorocarbon solvents 126
chromium, hexavalent 123
Church
  Austin 14, 18, 47
  Elihu 18, 19, 29, 48
  James 18, 50
Church & Co. 18
Church & Dwight Co. 51, 101
Chris Rutt 28
circuit boards 126
clay subsoils 112
Clinton College 11
Clutterbuck, Lady Maria 22
coating wastes 123
coffee 37
Cogswell & Crane 10

cold oven baking 148
Colgate-Palmolive 101
compressed yeast 20, 27, 143
Conant, James 8
consumer demand 39
contaminated soils 127
corn flour 139, 140
corrosive water 112
Count Rumford 8, 28
cow, dairy 105
Cow Brand 19, 29, 31, 44, 46, 48, 51
cream of tartar 20, 26, 27, 98, 142, 148
credit 33
Crowell, Luther Childs 31
Crowfield, Christopher 22
cryolite 47
Cullen, Michael 41

dairy cow 176
Davis Milling Co. 29
DDT 129
decorated tins 31
Deland & Co. 47
Dental Care toothpaste 101
dentifrice 101
deodorizers 58
depainting aircraft 125
Depression 40
detergency 57
dicalcium phosphate dihydrate 98
dieldrin 129
Dietetic Saleratus 47
dioxins 121
disease
  gum 102
  periodontal 102
distillers 10
distribution, retail 34
Dr. Miles Compound Extract of Tomato 45
dried yeast 20
dry injection 119, 120
dry carbonation 7, 9, 16, 49
dry phosphate of lime 26
Duke of Orleans 6
duodenal fluid ii
durum wheat 135
Dwight, Mrs. 22
Dwight, John 16, 31, 43
Dwight & Co., John 17, 19
Dwight's Saleratus 17, 18, 22, 43

Eben Horsford 26
Economy Store 38
Edison, Thomas 26
effervescence 57

oat flour 139, 140
Oliver Evans 5
organic acid flux 126
organic sludge 122
organic wastes 122
ozone depleting chemicals 126

packaged goods 31, 33
packaging 31, 52
packaging technology 31
paint stripping 123
paper bag 31
  machine 31
  self-opening 31
  square bottom 31
particulate emissions 120
Pasteur, Louis 26
Patterson, Dr. James 114
Patton, William 47
Paul Keyes, Dr. 102
4-PCH 126
Peak toothpaste 101
pearlash 4, 10, 14
Pearline 47
PennSalt 47, 49
Pennsylvania Salt Manufacturing Co. 18, 19, 47
pentachlorophenol 128
periodontal disease 102
periodontists 104
Periogene 104
peroxide, hydrogen 103
pesticides, halogenated 127, 129
pH 56
Philadelphia Centennial Exposition 19
Philo Penfield Stewart 25
phosphoric acid 27
Piggly Wiggly 40
Pittsburgh Plate Glass Co. 50
plaque 101, 102
  acids 105
  bacterial 102
plastic media blasting 125
polychlorinated
  biphenyls (PCBs) 128
  dibenzofurans 129
  dibenzo-p-dioxins 129
potash 4, 11
  embargo 4
  Russian 4
potassium
  bicarbonate 7
  bromate 136
  carbonate 4
  iodate 136
  saleratus 10

potato water 13
power plants 119
prepared foods 99
Preston & Merrill baking powder 20, 27
private label brands 35
private label suppliers 38
Prophy-Jet 124
pulverulent phosphoric acid 27
Pyle, James 46

quinoa flour 141

railroads
  Central Pacific 29
  Union Pacific 29
railworkers 30
ranges, wood burning 8
Read, Nathan 9
recipe booklets 44
recipes
  breakfast
    cornmeal pancakes 164
    English muffin loaves 165
    funnel cakes 165
    graham buttermilk pancakes 163
    orange raisin scones 163
    waffles 164
  cookies
    big & easy oatmeal cookies 158
    birthday cookie 159
    bran apple bars 162
    chocolate peanut butter cookies 161
    orange apricot cookies 160
    peanut butter chocolate cookies 161
    toll house redux 160
  desserts
    almond pound cake 170
    banana chip cake 167
    chocolate glaze 170
    cranberry cake 166
    fudge frosting 169
    really chocolate cake 168
    really really chocolate cake 169
    sour cream pound cake 167
    yogurt glaze 167
  quick breads & muffins
    apple nut muffins 156
    banana oat raisin muffins 158
    brown bread muffins 157
    buttermilk amaranth/corn bread 153
    date nut bread 151
    eggplant/zucchini bread 154
    harvest bread 153
    nouvelle corn bread 155
    old-fashioned corn bread 152